Mastering the Art of Decoding DSM-5

Claytonz H. Baker

Funny helpful tips:

In the mountains of challenges, scale new heights with determination and grit.

Avoid letting external pressures dictate your relationship's pace.

Mastering the Art of Decoding DSM-5 : Unlocking the Secrets of DSM-5: The Comprehensive Guide to Expertly Analyze Mental Disorders

Life advices:

Stay open to revising your opinions; a well-argued book can offer new perspectives and change minds.

Your story is continuously unfolding; be the author of your destiny, not just a passive observer.

Introduction

Welcome to the world of the DSM-5 (Fifth Edition), a vital tool in the field of mental health and psychology. This audio study guide is your companion in understanding the complexities of this manual, providing a comprehensive overview of its contents, including diagnostic criteria, disorders, and important considerations.

In this journey through the DSM-5, we'll delve into various aspects of mental health and diagnosis. From cautionary statements regarding forensic use to the exploration of personality disorders and neurodevelopmental conditions, this guide is your gateway to comprehending the DSM-5's invaluable contributions to the mental health field.

As we navigate through the diverse range of disorders and criteria outlined in the DSM-5, you'll gain insights into the intricacies of mental health assessment, diagnosis, and treatment. Whether you're a student, clinician, or someone with a keen interest in psychology, this guide aims to enhance your understanding and application of the DSM-5's principles.

Our journey begins with an exploration of the cautionary statement regarding the forensic use of the DSM-5. We'll emphasize the ethical considerations and responsibilities associated with employing this manual in legal contexts.

Next, we'll venture into the realm of personality disorders, including discussions on Narcissistic Personality Disorder, Antisocial Personality Disorder, Borderline Personality Disorder, and Schizotypal Personality Disorder. These conditions are significant contributors to the field of psychology and warrant thorough examination.

Our exploration continues with an in-depth look at specific disorders, such as Brief Psychotic Disorder, Schizophreniform Disorder, Schizophrenia, Schizoaffective Disorder, and Bipolar Disorder. We'll unravel the diagnostic criteria and key characteristics of these conditions.

Moving forward, we'll delve into neurodevelopmental disorders, including Intellectual Disabilities, Intellectual Development Disorder, Communication Disorders, and Attention Deficit Hyperactivity Disorder (ADHD). Understanding these conditions is vital in providing appropriate care and support.

We'll also explore motor disorders, such as Developmental Coordination Disorder, Stereotyped Movement Disorder, and Tic Disorders, including Tourette's Disorder and Persistent (Chronic) Motor or Vocal Tic Disorder. These conditions may present unique challenges in diagnosis and management.

Our journey will encompass Substance/ Medication-Induced Psychotic Disorder, Catatonia, and Anxiety Disorders, including Agoraphobia and Obsessive-Compulsive Disorder (OCD). We'll examine their diagnostic criteria and treatment approaches.

Furthermore, we'll delve into Dissociative Disorders, which can manifest in various ways, and explore Sexual Disorders, gaining insights into their diagnostic criteria.

Lastly, we'll discuss the alternative DSM-5 model for personality disorders and examine Major Depressive Episode, a pivotal component in mood disorder diagnoses.

Throughout this audio study guide, we aim to provide a comprehensive understanding of the DSM-5's content and its significance in mental health diagnosis and treatment. Whether you're seeking academic enrichment, professional growth, or a deeper understanding of mental health, we're here to guide you on this informative journey through the DSM-5.

So, let's embark on this illuminating voyage into the world of mental health and the DSM-5, where we'll gain the knowledge and insights to make a positive impact on the lives of individuals seeking mental well-being and healing.

Contents

Cautionary Statement for Forensic Use of DSM-5

The concept of capacity is not separated from the previous one, considering the ability, suitability and legal capacity of a person to own and exercise a civil, political or administrative right or function. This is considered in two modalities: legal capacity, when it comes to the aptitude to be active or passive subject of legal relationships, and legal capacity, which designates the aptitude or faculty to exercise them.

The legal capacity is achieved by the mere fact of being a person, when a new being is born; it is total, immutable, of public order, it does not have any type of restriction or limitation, it is the subject by its own right, the right to exist, and therefore it is also known as the ability to enjoy.

Upon reaching the age of majority, legal capacity is acquired, which allows the subject not only to be the owner, to exercise or demand rights, to contract obligations in a personal manner and to appear at trial, but to modify or extinguish legal relationships voluntarily and autonomously. This is the ability to act, which is supported by the will understood as the psychic faculty that considers, plans, chooses and finally approves to perform or not a certain act; the will is closely related to the desire and intention to perform a particular act or event.

The ability to act or exercise capacity is a legal quality that determines the effectiveness of the acts performed by a person according to their civil conditions; it is the possibility of acting in life according to requirements. It is also defined as the ability to constitute, modify or extinguish public relations, and therefore is the ideal to perform legal acts.

In this way, the ability to act is an acquisition, or better, a faculty given by the State, which is attributed to the person who meets requirements such as, for example, the age of majority; therefore, the same State may limit, restrict or withdraw it, according to specific circumstances regulated by the legal regime; in this sense, in the final part of article 1502 of Book Four of the Civil Code (CC), pronounces on requirements to acquire obligations and contracts:

ARTICLE 1502. Requirements to Compromise. For a person to be forced to another by an act or declaration of will, it is necessary:

1o.) That is legally capable.

2o.) That consents in said act or declaration and its consent does not suffer from vice.

3o.) That falls on a lawful object.

4th) that has a lawful cause.

The legal capacity of a person then, is to be able to oblige by itself, without the ministry or the authorization of another.

A person, to acquire obligations or contract, in addition to knowing the object and the consequences derived from said act, must have and declare the will to do so, freely consent; This means, therefore, possess psychological qualities that allow him to act independently and be autonomous in making decisions. This constitutes what the legislator calls the legal capacity of a person, or "to be able to obligate himself, without the ministry or the authorization of another." This aptitude to be a holder of rights or legal duties is presumed by the Colombian State in all its associates, as stipulated in Article 1503 of the CC:

ARTICLE 1503. Presumption of Capacity. Every person is legally capable, except those that the law declares incapable.

The capacity to act may be total or partial, according to certain personal conditions such as age or marital status; this allows to enable people to perform all or only certain acts. In that sense, the ability to act is unequal, heterogeneous, different in one person and another, and may even vary in the same person according to the situation in which he finds himself. The capacity to act is not determined solely by knowledge or natural reason, but by this and the particular relationships established with the civil and legal conditions of each individual; in this way, for example, an active member of the Armed Forces can make employment or purchase contracts, but cannot elect or be elected in public corporations.

While the legal capacity contemplates the subject in a static position, relative to the enjoyment, enjoyment or possession of rights, the ability to act focuses the subject from an essentially dynamic angle, since it refers to the acquisition and transmission of rights. This mutability prevents the existence of an absolute and perennial capacity to act, although it admits a full capacity that corresponds to nationals of legal age without legal impediments, who can perform all acts of civil life, except those expressly exempted by law (capacity). full, but not absolute). The capacity to act admits limitations, as happens with the minority of age, or it can be modified when the state interdiction proceeds, for which it is obliged to mediate a particular legal act.

Considering that the ability to act is based on decision making and vice versa, is not subject to limitations, and therefore the individual is free to choose between a lawful and unlawful decision. The first is protected by law, there the action falls on a lawful object and has a lawful cause, which refers to the ability to do business and is called negotiating capacity The second, rejected by law and consisting of the possibility of commit crimes, is the criminal capacity (Valencia-Zea, & Ortiz-Monsalve, 2002).

Mental Disability

Although the text of Law 1306 of 2009 does not specify the meaning of incapacity or disability, the spirit of the Law aims to protect those persons who, due to the effects of congenital pathology, hereditary or not, due to disorders acquired after birth or due to difficulties related to health, they are immersed in the concepts that she contemplates. In no way does it include those who, due to the biological immaturity of their age, have not yet been able to achieve the full use of their legal capacities, such as mentally healthy children, as well as all mentally ill children.

Therefore, disability and disability are terms that merit conceptualization from the forensic sciences, specifically from forensic psychiatry; these disciplines have for them a specific meaning and a broad development that includes biological, psychological and socio-environmental aspects.

Forensic Concept of Mental Disability

The legal relationships that generate the origin of the State are established between subjects able to act autonomously, who do not require authorization from another person to acquire obligations, or in other words, who are capable; therefore, those who do not possess these qualities are the exception, and the State and its partners assume their protection from a court ruling that declares them legally incompetent, as specified or clarified in Article 1504 of the CC:

ARTICLE 1504. Absolute and Relative Disability. The insane, the impubic and deaf-mute, who cannot be understood in writing, are absolutely incapable.

Their acts do not produce even natural obligations, and do not admit caution.

In addition to these disabilities there are other particulars that consist in the prohibition that the law has imposed on certain people to execute certain acts.

From the above it follows that, as an exception, to be sanctioned as a legal disability must be proven in a judicial process. Therefore, to have objective bases to establish or prove their existence, it is necessary to define disability conceptually and operationally, in order that, in due course, the judge may use said concept to decree it in cases that merit it.

In a first approximation, the term incapacity must be understood as the non-existence of capacity, either by loss, by significant diminution of independence or by requiring help or authorization from a capable person; In this way, the task is to prove the non-capacity derived from the absence, reduction, excess or distortion of mental functions, a scientific work entrusted to forensic psychiatry.

Now, while the CC uses the term incapacity, Law 1306 of 2009 uses the term mental disability and prohibits the use of the demented phrase:

ARTICLE 2. Subjects with mental disabilities: A natural person has mental disability when he suffers from psychic or behavioral limitations, which does not allow him to understand the scope of his acts or assume excessive or unnecessary risks in the management of his patrimony.

The legal incapacity of people with mental disabilities will be correlated to their affectation, without prejudice to the bargaining security and the right of third parties acting in good faith.

PARAGRAPH. The term "insane" that currently appears in the other laws, will be understood replaced by "person with mental disability" and in the valuation of their acts, the provisions of this law will apply as pertinent.

Thus, Law 1306 of 2009 defines disability according to the limitation that a person presents, a position also accepted by the Mental Health Law (Colombia, Congress of the Republic, 2013), which defines it as follows:

ARTICLE 5. Definitions. For the application of this law, the following definitions shall be taken into account:

Mental disability - It occurs in a person who suffers from psychic or behavioral limitations; that they do not allow him to understand the scope of his actions on multiple occasions, he has difficulty performing actions or tasks, and to participate in life situations. The mental disability of an individual can be presented in a transitory or permanent manner, which is defined under clinical criteria of the treating medical team.

Both regulations coincide in considering mental disability as a limitation that can be psychic or behavioral, which, as a central axis, does not allow us to understand the scope of the acts. In that sense, mental disability has two conditions: nature and result. The nature refers to the disability itself, which occur when the subject suffers "limitations", whether "psychic" or "behavior", and this is defined as the continent; On the other hand, the result or content is the legal incapacity attributed by the legislator.

The nature of the mental disability is eminently psychopathological, since the subject is required to present and maintain one or more alterations in their functions or in their bodily structures that generate psychic or behavioral limitations, without considering the etiology or cause of these ; that the pathology is hereditary, congenital or acquired does not matter, but simply that it exists and produces a result.

The content, given by the legal result of one or both limitations, together with other factors related to health and personal and contextual factors, prevents or hinders in much understanding the scope of the acts and leads the subject to -or provides- take excessive or unnecessary risks in the patrimonial management, to the point that the person with mental disability would be prevented from noticing the consequences of their actions in general and making contracts or business, including, of course, the management of their assets. This component refers to the "legal incapacity of persons with mental disabilities" indicated in the article in question, which -continues the rule- is in correlation with the affectation, without prejudice to the negotiating security and the right of third parties that they act in good faith; these last aspects are only of legal nature.

Based on the annotation, it can be stated, in a schematic way, that the disability includes:

Nature:

- Psychic limitations

- Behavioral limitations

Mental disability

Consequences:

- Inability to warn the extent of acts

- Assumption of excessive or unnecessary risks

- Difficulty to execute actions or tasks and to participate in life situations

Legal incapacity

In the second paragraph of article 2, the Law states that "the legal incapacity of persons with mental disabilities shall be correlative to their affectation"; This approach allows us to point out, first of all, that legal disability is a legal attribute of mental disability and coexists with it because it is its product; and second, that being "correlative to its affectation", the legislator admits different degrees of both mental disability and legal incapacity, precisely because of their coexistence. Therefore, for purposes of the Law under study, the disability is subsumed in the disability, which makes the concept more operative, since the disability is not homogeneous, and both it and the disability have levels, categories or modalities; For that reason, for practical purposes, mutatis mutandis, what the CC calls disability, Law 1306 of 2009 denominates disability.

The expression "assumption of excessive or unnecessary risks" also requires an approach from the perspective of psychopathology; it includes the difficulty of the person to grasp reality, discern and foresee the consequences of their decisions. It is not in this case the mental processes involved in opting for equivocal measures or behavior, either by absence or insufficient information, by mistake, by inappropriate vision of commercial possibilities, or even by those determined by other processes closer to the vital dysfunctionality or personality, such as greed, greed, selfishness, immoderation, submission, caprice, excessive caution, envy, intrigue, illegality, etc.

It is impossible to stop commenting that the abolition of the demented term, historically consecrated in the CC, and its replacement by the person with mental disability, constitutes an important advance in the legislation. In this way, among other aspects, confusion is avoided both with the medical term, which has a diagnostic character for a specific group of diseases, dementias, and with the popular term pejorative meaning.

Qualification of the mental disability

Although qualification and classification are correlated, first the qualification of an event is expected to later classify it if it is pertinent; Thus, in article 17, the legislator generates the concept of absolute mental disability and then addresses the issue of disability qualification in general:

ARTICLE 17. The Subject with Absolute Mental Disability. Those who suffer from a severe or profound condition or pathology of learning, behavior or mental deterioration are considered to be totally mentally disabled.

The qualification of the disability will be made following the scientific parameters adopted by the National Consultative Committee of People with Limitations and using an internationally accepted nomenclature.

Criteria and qualification mechanisms are not specified, and yet, in the second section, the need to use scientific parameters is established, and for this reason, the National Consultative Committee of People with Restrictions is delegated to determine or adopt the corresponding scientific criteria.. This Committee was created by means of Decree 730 of 1995 of the Presidency of the Republic, initially with the name of the National Consultative Committee on Disability:

ARTICLE 1o. The National Advisory Committee on Disability is created, attached to the Ministry of Health, as an advisory body to the Vice Presidency of the Republic, for issues related to disability in all areas of economic and social activity in the country.

ARTICLE 2o. Objective. This Advisory Committee will be an advisor, for the establishment of a culture of respect for the dignity and improvement of the quality of life of the disabled population; promoting awareness of the State, society and family, around the reality of disability and the importance for the country of the development of activities that favor the social and economic integration of this population.

Law 361 of 1997 establishes the mechanisms of social integration of persons with disabilities and replaces the Committee mentioned by the National Consultative Committee of Persons with Disabilities; This was regulated by Decree 1068 of 1997 of the Presidency of the Republic, and in turn was modified by Decree 276 of 2000, which states its quality, nature, functions and structure:

ARTICLE 1o. Conformation. The National Consultative Committee of People with Restrictions is a body, permanent institutional adviser, to monitor and verify the implementation of policies, strategies and programs that ensure the social integration of the limited, will be coordinated by the Ministry Presidential for Social Policy and conformed.

Subsequently, Article 6 of Law 361 of 1997, which created the National Consultative Committee of People with Disabilities, was repealed by Law 1145 of 2007, through which the National Disability System was organized, and the National Advisory Committee was created of Persons in Disability Situation.

To fulfill its functions, the National Consultative Committee of People with Limitations, within its powers and in consideration of international agreements accepted by Colombia, accepted the content of Resolution WHA54.21 of the World Health Organization, adopted by the Fifty-fourth World Health Assembly in May 2001, which states that the WHO:

1. ENDORSES the second edition of the International Classification of Deficiencies, Disabilities and Disabilities (CIDDM), with the title "International Classification of Functioning, Disability and Health", hereinafter abbreviated as CIF;

2. URGES Member States to use, as appropriate, GIF in their research, monitoring and notification activities, taking into account specific situations in Member States and, in particular, in view of possible future revisions.

The main objective of the GIF is "to provide a conceptual framework based on scientific, for the understanding and study of health and related states, its results and determinants, in addition to establishing a unified and standardized language to the underlying challenges". The authors refer that the CIF should be considered as a complement to the International Classification of Diseases 10th revision (ICD-10) of the World Health Organization (WHO), which in chapter V deals with mental disorders.

Therefore, the National Advisory Committee of People with Limitations adopted as scientific parameters to qualify disability, the International Classification of Functioning, Disability and Health, known by the acronym CIF (WHO & OPS, 2000), and the

International Classification of Diseases 10th revision, whose acronym is ICD-10.

International Classification of Diseases: ICD-10

The activity of classifying is a necessary act in global human functioning and essential for the understanding and development of science; in medicine allows the systematic registration of information, analysis, interpretation and comparison of data related to health and disease in human groups and pathology categories, generated according to established criteria regarding affected organs, etiology, clinical presentation, severity, evolution, among others. In psychiatry, the two most important classifications are the International Classification of Diseases (ICD) established by the WHO and the Statistical Manual of Mental Illnesses (DSM) prepared by the American Psychiatric Association; both classifications are subject to periodic revision and updating.

The International Classification of Diseases 10th revision (ICD-10) considers, unifies and standardizes diagnostic terms, and creates universal alphanumeric codes that allow easy storage and retrieval for information analysis.

The ICD-10 is a decimal classification of international diagnoses for epidemiological purposes, health management and clinical use, which is used at different levels of care, provides the conceptual framework for the classification of diseases and serves as the basis for the Member States of WHO for the codification and compilation of national mortality and morbidity statistics; for these it has official character. The WHO is currently working on the 11th revision.

The ICD-10 is made up of 21 chapters and includes current knowledge about diseases and health conditions. The alphanumeric codes allow to expand or reduce the classification according to the development of science and the discovery of new health conditions or the etiology of the disease. The fifth chapter, marked with the F code, corresponds to mental and behavioral disorders; it is organized into ten sections, each one for each diagnostic class, which begins its notation with the letter F, and immediately after that numbers are used; the first four digits of the code have official international status, the fifth and sixth digits are destined for regional adaptation according to their particular local conditions, and the first digit signifies the diagnostic category. In this way, a decimal classification is obtained that allows having a thousand diagnostic categories and perform multiaxial diagnosis in which the main category of mental affectation is included, its organic conditions, severity, social and environmental conditions.

The groups of mental and behavioral disorders of the ICD-10 are:

F0: Mental and organic disorders including symptomatic.

Fl: Mental and behavioral disorders due to the consumption of psychotropic substances.

F2: Schizophrenia, schizotypal disorder and related psychotic disorders.

F3: Mood disorders (affective).

F4: Neurotic disorders, stress-related disorders and somatoform disorders.

F5: Behavioral syndromes associated with physiological alterations and physical factors.

F6: Personality and behavior disorders in adults.

F7: Mental retardation.

F8: Disorders of psychological development.

F9: Emotional and behavioral disorders that usually appear in childhood and adolescence.

Classification of mental disorders according to the DSM

In many countries of the world the Diagnostic and Statistical Manual of Mental Disorders (known by the acronym DSM by its name in English: Diagnostic and Statistical Manual of Mental Disorders) is used, elaborated and published by the American Psychiatric Association (2013). The 5th revision, the DSM-5, which uses codes similar to those of the ICD-10, is currently in force, despite the fact that certain disorders are denominated differently or have some non-shared diagnostic criteria. This is the official classification in the United States, adapted to the needs and sanitary requirements and of the insurance companies of that country.

The DSM-5 has a descriptive vision; contains the following 22 chapters of clinical description:

1. Disorders of neurological development.

2. Spectrum of schizophrenia and other psychotic disorders.

3. Bipolar disorder and related disorders.

4. Depressive disorders.

5. Anxiety disorders.

6. Obsessive compulsive disorder and related disorders.

7. Disorders related to traumas and stress factors.

8. Dissociative disorders.

9. Disorder of somatic symptoms and related disorders.

10. Eating disorders and the ingestion of food.

11. Disorders of excretion.

12. Sleep and wakefulness disorders.

13. Sexual dysfunctions.

14. Gender dysphoria.

15. Destructive disorders of impulse and behavior control.

16. Disorders related to stays and addictive disorders.

17. Neurocognitive disorders.

18. Personality disorders.

19. Paraphilic disorders.

20. Other mental disorders.

21. Motor disorders induced by medications and other adverse drug factors.

22. Other problems that may be subject to clinical attention.

Because the diagnostic criteria and text of the DSM-5 are intended for clinical evaluation, case formulation, and a treatment plan, a warning or "cautionary statement" is issued for forensic use:

Accordingly, it is important to note that the definition of mental disorder contained in the DSM-5 was written to meet the needs of clinicians, public health professionals, and researchers, rather than the technical needs of courts and professionals.

This recommendation is also valid for ICD-10; from there derives, among other aspects, the importance of the forensic subspecialty in psychiatry to explore, diagnose and explain what refers to mental disorders and the behavior of people linked to legal processes.

However, it is necessary to be clear that, on the basis of international agreements signed and adopted as part of the country's legal system, the International Statistical Classification of Diseases and Related Health Problems, in its 10th revision, ICD-10, is the official classification.

International Classification of Functioning,

Disability and Health: CIF

The International Classification of Functioning, Disability and Health (corneamente acronym with the acronym CIF) arises from an international effort in which Colombia participated. It describes and compares the health status of the populations, not only on the basis of morbidity and mortality, as has traditionally been done, but from the concept of burden of disease; this consists in measuring the loss of health attributable to illnesses and injuries or to the associated risk factors and determinants, to the point that all diseases have the same importance as generators of disability, regardless of their cause.

By including the states related to health in its conceptual framework, it studies the human being in his family, social and geographical environment, which allows to expand the disability vision, since, without being the people the classification unit, describes his situation individual in a contextualized way. To this end, the CIF calls the descriptors of the health domain of health, and the components of health-relevant health-related domains. In this way it maintains a broad concept of health, and although the definition does not cover some circumstances caused by socioeconomic factors, it is valid for all people, since it does not only refer to people with disabilities. It is made up of two parts:

1. Function and disability.
2. Contextual factors.

The first part, "Functioning and disability", is constituted by the component of the body, which includes the functions of the corporal systems and structures of the body, and by the component of activities and participation; These cover aspects related to functioning from an individual and social perspective. They can be used to indicate problems (deficiencies, limitation of activity or restriction in participation) included under the global concept of disability, or to describe non-problematic aspects of health or in relation to it, included in the generic concept of functioning.

The second part, "Contextual Factors", is a list of environmental factors that exert an effect on all components of functioning and disability, which range from the context / immediate environment of the individual to the general environment. Although it includes personal factors, these are not classified in the CIF "due to the great social and cultural variability associated with them".

To make the approach more intelligible, the theoretical corpus of the CIF defines bodily functions as those physiological functions of bodily systems (including psychological ones); and with body structures refers to the anatomical constitution of the organism. Alterations in bodily functions or structures, such as a significant deviation or loss, produce deficiency; This is not equivalent to pathology, because its concept is broader than that of disease and can be detected by direct observation or by inference from that observation, sometimes with the help of instruments.

Concerning the concurrent activity-participation, the activity is the realization of a task or action by an individual, while participation is the act of getting involved in a vital situation. The limitations are conceived as the difficulties that a person can have in the performance / realization of the activities. Restrictions on participation are problems that someone may experience when involved in life situations. The functioning and disability of a person are conceived by the CIF as a dynamic interaction, either as a process or result of health conditions (illnesses, disorders, injuries, etc.) and of personal and environmental contextual factors, such as the physical environment, social or attitudinal.

According to well-defined criteria, deficiencies are classified into categories by loss or absence, reduction, increase or excess and deviation; once deficiencies are present, they can be graded in terms of severity: mild or severe; temporary, permanent or fluctuating in time; progressive, regressive or static; intermittent or continuous. The CIF considers that the disability must be defined by professionals trained to judge the physical and mental functioning according to the current level of knowledge, excluding for practical reasons the molecular level, without considering the etiology or the way to develop. It recommends the use of evaluation instruments in order to identify and quantify the degree of performance limitation in relation to accepted standards in the population, and to achieve the integration of the different dimensions of functioning.

Legal effects of the mental disability

Mental disability, broadly understood as a deficit in the psychological functioning of a person, generates a response of protection in the State through legal provisions, which are supported by the provisions of articles 2, 15 and 16 of Law 1306 of 2009, whose texts are recalled below:

ARTICLE 2. Subjects with Mental Disability A natural person has mental disability when he suffers from psychic or behavioral limitations, which does not allow him to understand the scope of his acts or assume excessive or unnecessary risks in the management of his patrimony.

The legal incapacity of people with mental disabilities will be correlated to their affectation, without prejudice to the bargaining security and the right of third parties acting in good faith.

PARAGRAPH. The term "insane" that currently appears in the other laws, will be understood replaced by "person with mental disability" and in the valuation of their acts, the provisions of this law will apply as pertinent.

ARTICLE 15. Legal capacity of the subjects with Disability. Those who suffer from absolute mental disability are absolutely incapable. The subjects with relative mental disability, disqualified according to this law, are considered incapable relative with respect to those acts and businesses on which the disqualification rests. In the rest it will be the general rules of capacity.

ARTICLE 16. Acts of other Persons with Disabilities. The assessment of the validity and effectiveness of actions taken by those who suffer temporary disorders that affect their lucidity and are not subject to protective measures will continue to be governed by the ordinary rules.

On the basis of the direct relationship between mental capacity and legal capacity, it is explicitly stated that legal incapacity derives from mental disability; it is a situation of exception that obliges, according to the block of constitutionality, that the legal effect of the mental deficit must be established through a judicial process by competent authority. For this, it is necessary to prove the presence of mental disability through a careful expert examination by forensic psychiatry, where the conditions and mental capacities of the committed are evaluated; this in order to find clinical elements that allow to determine the existence of a mental alteration that sustains said disability, and determine its characteristics and modality to establish, from the perspective of psychiatry, what is indicated by the law as "correlative to its affectation" .

This article uses or generates a series of technical terms that will be clarified as it continues in its study. In that sense, Article 15 states that the person suffering from absolute mental disability acquires the status of absolute incapacitated. Similarly, when the judge meets people with relative mental disabilities, relative disability is predicated. It is then that mental disability is a diagnosis of forensic psychiatry and disability is a legal qualification.

The absolute term means commitment of the totality of mental functions and legal capacity; on the other hand, the relative word is synonymous with partial, sectoral or in relation to; in this case, the disability is considered "only with respect to those acts and businesses on which the disqualification rests". Thus, the forensic diagnosis of relative mental disability refers to an area of mental functioning, which for forensic study must be specified by the authority when it requests the expert opinion, according to which its legal effect is the inability.

For practical purposes, the forensic surgeon, when defining the presence of relative mental disability, describes the deficit area or function based on the legal needs of the process; In turn, the judge must specify the particular area (s) to be examined regarding capacity, or perhaps better, determine in which specific areas or for which performance skills and abilities it is required to assess non-capacity of the subject.

Modalities of Mental Disability

Article 2 states that "the legal incapacity of persons with mental disabilities will be correlated to their affectation", considering that the mental disability is not unique, uniform or "universal", but on the contrary, heterologous, changing and has plasticity. These properties allow to establish different forms and categories or modalities of mental disability, according to the mental functions affected in relation to its extension, severity and other evolutionary characteristics of the affectation that determines it, as well as the particularities of the person and the environment. in which that develops.

In this way, the mental disability can adopt different modalities according to the psychopathological characteristics of the injury, in relation to:

The invasive: refers to the quality and quantity of mental functions that effect or affect the mental apparatus; It can be superficial if it invades few functions, or deep if it covers a large part of the mental apparatus or includes the intellect-cognitive or the executive.

The extension or amplitude: it could be total if it covers the complete function, or partial if it is committed only in some level or grade of it.

The origin: the cause or etiology of the lesion is congenital if it is acquired during the gestational period, whether it is hereditary or not, and it is acquired if it is after that period, whether it is traumatic, infectious, toxic, metabolic, etc.

Presentation: is the way the disease starts, depending on whether it is sudden or slowly and progressively.

Evolution (or historical development): can be of relative short duration or acute or evolve into long or chronic time.

The nature of the process: it leads to its transitoriness or final installation.

Temporality: is given by the presence and sequence of events (episode, crisis, cycles, state).

Therapeutic response: refers to the possibility or not and proper response of the mental affectation, not of the entity that originates it; it would be reversible if the mental functions improve, or on the contrary, irreversible, permanent or definitive if this is not possible.

The family or social environment: either functional or dysfunctional, directly affects the psychopathology of the person.

Prognosis: refers to the possibility or not of improvement, and in that sense can be reversible (favorable) or irreversible (unfavorable).

The severity: determined by the intensity or depth of the injury, is directly related to the other characteristics and generates the levels of severity: mild, moderate or severe.

Legal consolidation: sufficient evolutionary permanence and significant impact of the environment that determines a legal meaning or significance.

There are, then, at least 12 indicators that record the nature of mental disability and give guidelines for its classification:

1. Invasiveness: superficial, profound

2. Extension: total, partial

3. Origin: congenital, acquired

4. Presentation: sudden, insidious

5. Evolution: acute, chronic

6. Character: transitory, definitive

7. Temporality: episode, crisis, cycles, state

8. Therapeutic response: reversible, irreversible

9. Socio Familiar environment: functional, dysfunctional

10. Prognosis: favorable, unfavorable

11. Severity: mild, moderate, severe

12. Legal consolidation: evolutionary permanence

The interaction of these factors generates particularities in mental illness, to the extent that, insofar as it is total or partial, permanent or transitory, reversible or irreversible, etc., criteria are obtained to catalog the nature of the mental disability and determine its absolute or relative modality, in accordance with the provisions of article 15:

ARTICLE 15. Legal capacity of the subjects with Disability. Those who suffer from absolute mental disability are absolutely incapable. The subjects with relative mental disability, disqualified according to this law, are considered incapable relative with respect to those acts and businesses on which the disqualification rests. In the rest it will be the general rules of capacity.

In either of these two cases the limitation must achieve a level of severity of sufficient severity, with an evolutionary permanence and significant impact of the environment, so that it may have legal significance or significance, in order to achieve what M. Castex calls "legal consolidation". regardless of whether its origin is hereditary, congenital or acquired, or that, at a certain time, it is of great medical, work or social importance.

However, a person may suffer from a very severe condition, and therefore very significant and limiting both clinically and occupationally, and even then, not constitute a cause of disability. For example, the sudden loss of a loved one generates a state of great psychological distress in the survivor and limits him in the development of his daily activities, but this yields in a progressive and natural way as the mourning is elaborated; this affliction has no legal significance beyond an incapacity for work; However, if the subject is not capable of mourning and this loss produces a serious, chronic mental impairment, which limits him to his free and cognitive actions, this limitation would achieve legal consolidation and could eventually be a reason for mental disability.

From the aforementioned it can be deduced that, since there are different modalities or varieties of mental disability, each one carries a specific legal consequence, namely:

Absolute mental disability = absolute disability

Relative mental disability = relative disability = non-skilled

Transient mental disability = temporary disorder that affects lucidity

Mental disability of the minor = absolute mental disability

According to article 2, as the psychic or behavioral limitation that prevents a subject from understanding the scope of their actions, or that impels them or allows them to assume excessive or unnecessary risks in the management of their assets, it must, insofar as a limitation is sufficiently extensive to engage most of the cognitive functions or at least the actual ability to use them, and also be of chronic evolution, should be considered a total limitation for the exercise of own decisions, thus configuring the absolute mental disability, which legally entails the quality of "absolute disability" according to or to the provisions of article 15.

Therefore, while absolute disability is a judicial decision, absolute mental disability is a forensic diagnosis from a condition of the subject beyond a mental impairment, because it constitutes the failure of their life situation that makes it impossible to capture the environment, be aware of the world of the real and owning yourself.

According to article 17, people with absolute mental disability are "those who suffer a severe or profound condition or pathology of learning, behavior or mental deterioration". As it was noticed, it is not of importance for the judge to know the origin of the affectation when making a decision in law; However, it is essential to know it in order to arrange medical treatment and other reparative or preventive mechanisms, as well as to avoid hereditary family affectations.

Relative mental disability

Article 15 provides that disability is relative when presented in relation to "those acts and businesses on which the disqualification rests. In the rest it will be to the general rules of capacity ". This legal concept is built on the conceptual basis that this type of disability is partial, correlative to the involvement of the performance areas that does not allow the subject to understand the scope of their actions, impel or expose them to excessive or unnecessary risks in the management of their heritage.

To support the assignment of the category "relative" to this type of disability, it is necessary to specify three terms: acts, business and disability, which will be addressed in chapter II of this book.

Other forms of disability

Chapter II of the Law under study, "Persons with Mental Disability", contains two articles: 15, which deals with the legal capacity of persons with disabilities, and 16, which deals with the actions of other persons with disability; the latter has:

ARTICLE 16. Acts of other persons with disabilities. The assessment of the validity and effectiveness of actions taken by those who suffer temporary disorders that affect their lucidity and are not subject to protective measures will continue to be governed by the ordinary rules.

The Law, by admitting the existence of "acts of other persons with disabilities", establishes a third type of mental disability. This occurs in people who suffer from severe alterations of the central nervous system that generate insufficiency in their global mental functioning, which temporarily affect their lucidity and therefore are potentially reversible ad integrum in a relatively short time, and which, for committing their autonomy to make decisions during that period, would result in transient mental disability.

On the other hand, it is necessary to consider that minors have limitations to exercise certain rights and legal obligations derived from the psychological immaturity proper to their age, and therefore they are subject to protective measures by the family, society and society. State, which become more specific when they suffer mental illnesses, especially if they alter their intellect-cognitive capacity.

Causes of mental disability

Because this is a psychiatric-forensic study, it is essential to start from the Law to apply and derive pertinent concepts and their categorization; In that order of ideas, according to article 2, mental disability is determined by two factors:

1. The psychic limitation.
2. The limitation of behavior.

Law 1306 of 2009, in article 28 (which will be studied later), accepts the medical nature of the disability and therefore of the limitation, when it is required to establish the nature of the disease, etiology, evolution and recommendations of management, in addition to determining the conditions of performance or performance. Accordingly, Article 659 of the Code of Civil Procedure (CPC), in the interdiction of persons with absolute mental disability, provides for an expert examination, which must include the clinical diagnosis, the etiology, the prognosis and the treatment to be performed. The legislator calls the person with a disability a patient, and orders that the opinion be made by a neurologist or psychiatrist to prove the presence of mental pathology, where the clinical characteristics are described, the diagnosis is established, its etiology or origin is explained, it is foreseen its evolution or prognosis and the therapeutic actions that the patient requires.

The legislator does not commit himself with medical, psychological, biological or etiological criteria to qualify the mental disability, but he poses it in a simple and broad manner as a limitation, which includes two attributes: impossibility to understand and ease to take unnecessary risks; it must be understood then as lack, insufficiency, lack, deterioration, impairment, although also as inconvenience, deviation, anomaly, alteration (Diccionario de la Lengua Española, 2005). Describes a circumstance or mental condition that restricts or hinders the development and performance of the person, as an impediment, defect or reduction of the possibilities of something. It has a pathological character insofar as it does not allow, hinder or distort a person's ability to achieve self-awareness or self-analysis and control of their mental activity, use knowledge and experiences to solve new problems and guide decision-making, anticipate results, select objectives , plan and formulate alternative solutions, select, initiate and maintain a response with control of its development in order to achieve the desired and avoid the harmful.

In pursuit of a psychiatric-forensic diagnosis, the psychopathology of the affectation must be considered, as it was stated in the section on mental disability modalities of this chapter, through at least 12 indicators that register the nature of the mental disability:

1. Invasiveness

2. Origin

3. Evolution

4. Temporality

5. Socio-family environment

6. Severity

7. Extension

8. Presentation

9. Character

10. Therapeutic response

11. Forecast

12. Legal consolidation

These elements make it possible to objectify and establish whether the limitation due to mental illness reaches legal representation, since it achieves legal significance as a mental disability. To do this, it must be sufficiently severe, prolonged, invasive, extensive, affect the subject and the environment, so that the person is not able to understand the consequences of their actions or anticipate excessive risks in the management of their assets; These qualities must be scientifically proven through expert examination.

The CIF, as a basic scientific norm, without ignoring the meaning and importance of the etiology of mental illness, dismisses the etiological aspects for the purposes of qualifying mental disability, since the essential thing is to demonstrate the presence of a detriment of mental functioning , or in other terms, the result of mental impairment or its impact on the intellect-cognitive and volitional functions of the person and their performance.

In this way, the aspects that allow the judge to have scientific elements strong enough to legally decree the legal incapacity as a result of the disability, provide for the protection of the integrity and health of the affected person, and protect their welfare and possibility of recovery, are eminently medical. Therefore, a physio pathological and psychopath genetic explanation of the psychic limitation and the limitation of the behavior is necessary, with respect to whether the alteration is congenital, hereditary or acquired due to infectious, traumatic, metabolic, toxic, autoimmune or other causes, as well as their interrelations with the social and family environment, and intra and interpersonal, given the psycho-social conditions of the human being.

Psychic Limitation

The psychic, in the context of Law 1306 of 2009, should be understood as the presence of global mental structures and faculties belonging to the intellect-cognitive domain and to the development and performance of the subject, which allow their autonomy, their self-determination. The psychic limitation refers to deficiency aspects determined by absence, loss or defect of said functions, which could reach pathological levels according to the extension, duration, depth or severity of the affectation, and in that sense, it is a concept of cut quantitative.

The human being in normal conditions is able to observe reality, pose problems, choose solutions and issue answers (correct or erroneous), thanks to a complex process of growth, development, maturation and integration, which begins in the intrauterine life and generates structures and functions that enable the existence of intelligent abstract behavior (Piaget, & Inhelder, 1971) (Bear,

Connors, & Paradiso, 1998). The subject with psychic limitation will then be the one to whom, for whatever reason, this process is lacking, and in whom it is impaired, interrupted, lost or distorted and makes it impossible to achieve adequate assimilation and accommodation before oneself and its surroundings, and fails in the adaptation to the environment. In this order of ideas, the limitation is constituted by three basic pathological processes:

1. Absence or impairment.

2. Loss.

3. Defect.

For forensic psychiatry, based on what is postulated by general psychopathology, the limited psychic is any person who presents a low level of intelligence and adaptive functioning due to absence, deficit or loss of intellectual-cognitive functions, either as a primary pathology or comorbidity. In this way, among other affectations, in the first group is, for example, the intellectual disability (DSM 5) or mental retardation (ICD-10); in the second group, the dementia syndromes, and in the third, the chronic psychoses and some severe non-psychotic affectations, as well as the generalized disorders of the development.

Intellectual disability (mental retardation)

For ICD-10 (WHO & OPS, 2000, p.184), mental retardation, coded as F700 to F799, is:

A disorder defined by the presence of an incomplete or detained mental development, characterized mainly by the deterioration of specific functions of each stage of development and that contribute to the overall level of intelligence, such as cognitive functions, those of language, the motor and socialization.

For the diagnosis of mental retardation, it is necessary to find: intelligence below the mean, with an intellectual quotient (IQ) close to 70-75 or lower; significant alteration of abilities or adaptive behavior and beginning before the age of 18. According to the DSM 5, three criteria must be fulfilled: deficiencies of the intellectual functions, confirmed by clinical evaluation and individualized standardized intelligence tests; deficiencies of adaptive behavior, and beginning of said intellectual and adaptive deficiencies during the development period.

The alteration of adaptive activity produces failure in the ability to achieve personal autonomy and social responsibility and limits the functioning in one or more activities of daily life, such as communication, social participation and independent living in any environment (family, school or social) (American Psychiatric Association, 2013).

In 2006 the then-American Association for Mental Retardation considered that, instead of mental retardation, the term intellectual disability should be used, taking into account that this mental pathology goes beyond a mere health problem, since it includes the lack of environmental support, and as a consequence the intellectual disability becomes noticeable to the extent that barriers appear in the environment. In coherence with the above, said association changed its name to the American Association on Intellectual and Developmental Disabilities, AAIDD (American Association of Intellectual and Developmental Disability).

Dementia Syndromes

Another of the large groups of mental disorders that generate limitations in psychic functions is that which corresponds to deficit disorders, dementia syndromes or simply dementias. These appear in subjects who, once they have achieved a normal intellectual-cognitive development, lose this capacity due to processes of different etiology. This alteration can occur at any time during adulthood (over 18 years of age), although it occurs more frequently in older adults.

For its part, the term dementia had a long and particular history in the legal environment; it was used in the CC, the CPC and many other legal provisions to refer to any form of alteration or mental dysfunction; fortunately it was disused with Law 1306 of 2009, because the paragraph of article 2 establishes that demented speech, in any norm, will be understood replaced by a person with a mental disability.

Dementia subsists as a medical term; in psychiatry it has a syndromic diagnostic character and belongs to the first group of ICD-10, "Organic Mental Disorders, including Symptomatic Disorders"; there it is defined as:

A syndrome due to a brain disease, usually chronic or progressive in nature, in which there is a deterioration of multiple higher cortical functions, among which are memory, thinking, orientation, understanding, calculation, the capacity for learning, language and judgment; the conscience is not clouded. Impairments in the cognitive area are often accompanied, and often preceded, by a deterioration of emotional control, social behavior or motivation.

In early stages, dementia pictures can present, rather than a true deficit, a deterioration of qualitative cognitive functions, and although to a lesser degree, it is still significant in relation to the usual efficiency with respect to the social behavior of the person. , personal care or the performance of familiar routines, by generating qualitative alterations of behavior.

Limitation of behavior

The expression limitations of behavior used by the legislator acquires a technical-conceptual connotation, and includes the mental dysfunctions that disturb the cognitive abilities that facilitate adaptation and the autonomous performance of the subject in new or complex situations that alter the overall capacity to understand and anticipate the scope of their actions, or that facilitate and allow the affected person to take excessive or unnecessary risks in the decision-making, including the management of their assets. The limitation, which in this case is qualitative and dynamic, refers to the distortion, damage or deformation of those psychological functions that allow the person to develop multiple and complex operations, such as the management of relationships with the surrounding reality; the regulation and control of trends and impulses; the processes of judgment and reasoning or synthetic function; defensive functions; the performance of autonomous functions, such as perception, thinking, intelligence and memory; the mediation between the internal world and external reality, as well as establishing its position in the world; and the coordination, generalization or simplification of data and psychic life.

In this perspective, behavior is the product or direct manifestation of the ability, skill and dexterity in the management of internal reality in relation to external reality, given by three aspects:

1. Sense of reality or awareness through the neurosensory device that allows the subject to differentiate the internal from the external of the Self.

2. Ability to discern between internal fantasies and external reality, that is, the faculty of evaluating reality.

3. Adaptation to the reality or ability of the subject to use their own resources in order to develop effective responses to the changing circumstances of life.

Among the pathologies included in this group are some dementias in their initial phase and psychosis in general, as well as some modalities of mood or affective disorders, especially bipolar disorders, mental disorders due to the use of psychoactive substances, serious neurotic disorders and impulse control, and mental alterations that affect mental functioning in a sectoral or partial manner without deconstructing the integrity of the ego.

Psychotic Syndromes

The psychotic is characterized by a significant deterioration of a person's ability to recognize and maintain contact with reality, relate and communicate with others and have an adequate affective response. This psychopathological situation is known as loss of the reality principle, and its origin is multifactorial and not completely elucidated until now; it is determined by a deep affectation in the personal and social functioning, and by the incapacity to perform the labor, school, home tasks, and daily demands in general; it entails regressive, extravagant and incoherent behavioral manifestations, and the affectation of multiple mental functions.

When there is a deterioration of the reality principle, people incorrectly evaluate their perceptions and thoughts and make erroneous inferences about the external world, even in the face of evidence to the contrary. The manifestation of psychotic behavior is the presence of delusions or hallucinations, with no criticism or introspection of its pathological nature; it includes badly disorganized behaviors, inappropriate, incoherent or incomprehensible language, and motor alterations that can lead to agitation. It forms a number of clinical pictures of psychiatric medical diagnosis, among which schizophrenias, paranoia, autism and organic mental disorders with psychosis stand out.

Mood Disorders (affective)

Mood disorders are characterized by affective instability impossible to regulate voluntarily, harmoniously and efficiently, which generates changes in daily life. These alterations tend to be chronic and recurrent, and involve not only affectivity, but perception, thought, memory and consciousness. The ICD-10 defines them as:

Disorders in which the fundamental disturbance consists of an alteration of mood or affect, which tends to depression (with or without concomitant anxiety), or euphoria. This change in mood is usually accompanied by changes in the general level of activity, and most of the other symptoms are secondary to these changes of mood and activity, or easily explained in the context of them.

Most of these disorders tend to be recurrent, and often the beginning of each episode is related to events or situations that generate stress.

They produce important social disruption, significant reduction of life expectancy and increase of lost years of labor and creative productivity. These alterations in mood are manifested by the presence of depressive episodes with deep sadness, apathy, loss of interest and feelings of disability with affect of motivation; or on the contrary, by phases of affective exaltation or mania, with hyperactivity, euphoria and ideas of greatness, which alternate in a different sequence and predominance between the depressive and manic poles; thus generate heterogeneous and recurrent frames of circular presentation, monopolar or bipolar, with intercortical lucidity periods of variable duration, even of very short duration, which in certain circumstances could significantly affect the judgment and reasoning and the ability to evaluate the reality, with restriction to discern and make autonomous decisions, through an adverse effect on the ability to develop critical functional abilities.

Impulse Control Disorders

These are behavioral disorders characterized by repetitive acts that do not have a clear rational motivation, which cannot be controlled, or partial control of them is achieved with great difficulty and psychological energy expenditure. They generally affect the interests of one's own person and of others. Behavior is associated with unstoppable desire or impulse to action, with a marked increase in psychic tension before the act, which may or may not be premeditated or planned, as with intermittent explosive disorder. In general, during the commission of the act, the subject presents a discharge of tension, gratification, pleasure and relaxation, followed by repentance, self-reproach and feelings of guilt; When the desire has been satisfied, the subject is aware that what has been done is harmful to him, his family or his community. This happens, for example, in the case of gambling, where the person has frequent episodes of play that dominate their lives and, while they are rewarding, they generate damage to their assets, their social, work and family obligations.

Impulse control disorders are specific to the conative sphere; they become the axis of the subject's life, who, knowing their harmful effects, establishes an internal struggle against them, giving themselves to satisfy the primary need, being practically impeded or at least severely limited their capacity for self-regulation and self-containment, to make decisions within reality, anticipate, plan, secure the future and act in accordance; Some of these alterations occur in cases of prodigality and dissipation.

Behavioral disorders due to brain injury

They are also known as organic mental disorders including symptomatic ones. In this nomination, organic refers to the fact that the disorders can be attributed to a dysfunction of cerebral or systemic disease diagnosable in itself; the symptomatic term is used to denote that the cerebral involvement is secondary to an extracerebral systemic disorder or disease. In this group there are clinical pictures with a wide variety of psychopathological manifestations that determine behavior alterations, whose evolution is influenced not only by biological elements, but also by personality, coping strategies, the social network and the economic and cultural level of the patient. In the initial phases, and according to the brain localization of the lesion, behavioral difficulties are generated that could be made visible by a greater legal than clinical meaning.

Other mental disorders

There are other situations that affect the ability to apprehend reality, make logical judgments, draw conclusions and make decisions in an autonomous and sensible way, given by the influence of psychoactive substances or by serious neurotic affectations that compromise, partially but profoundly , emotional functions, those related to the capacity of judgment and reasoning, as well as conatives. Among these disorders are some specific cases of:

Disorders derived from the consumption of psychoactive substances, on the understanding that these cause a direct activation of certain nuclei of the central nervous system located in the brain, especially the reward, which could determine behavioral alterations as a direct effect of consumption, or because the addictive substances induce, magnify or trigger certain psychotic, bipolar and other disorders.

Some specific modalities with a chronic character of dissociative disorders, in which there is partial or total loss of normal integration between certain memories of the past, awareness of one's own identity, some immediate sensations and control of bodily movements; may be determined by disturbance in intra and interpersonal relationships; Multiple personality cases can be included in this group.

Obsessive-compulsive disorder, characterized by the presence of ideas, images or impulses that penetrate and literally trap the patient's mind due to its reiterative and irrepressible nature; They are generally distressing in character and are accompanied by repetitive behaviors, sometimes very complex and useless, which are intended to prevent any event or damage caused to or by the patient.

Adaptive disorders may also be a cause of mental disability, insofar as a significant life change may generate a pathological reaction of a brief or prolonged depressive nature, or a disturbance of other emotions and behavior, that interfere with functioning and performance. social, by affecting the integrity of the network of social relationships of the person or the system of social foundations and values.

Not included in any group of mental pathology cases of commission of illegal or harmful acts in which there is clear intentionality or planning aimed at carrying them out, even with management of waiting time to give the right conditions to its realization; for example, concealed scams in an apparent gambling disorder or a dissociative disorder, where the actor simulates mental illness, nor when the person who commits the action, despite having mental illness, from the psychiatric field maintains the ability to understand and self-determine the commission of an unlawful act. In all these cases the mental functioning of the person who commits the action does not meet the criteria of mental disability.

Pervasive developmental disorders, perhaps the most severe, of the psychological development disorders described in ICD-10 with codes F80 to F89. The disorders included in this group have in common:

a) They invariably begin during childhood or childhood; b) there is deterioration or retardation of the development of functions closely related to the biological maturation of the central nevi system; c) they are of progressive course, without remissions or relapses. In most cases, the affected functions include language, visual-spatial abilities and motor coordination. Usually, delay or deterioration becomes apparent as soon as it can be reliably detected and progressively diminished as children grow up, although minor deficits often remain during adulthood.

Pervasive developmental disorders are characterized by a qualitative alteration of social interaction and forms of communication, and by a repetitive, stereotyped and restricted repertoire of interests and activities. These alterations can be global or affect specific areas, such as those related to mathematics, reading, writing, language, visuospatial functions or motor coordination, or also affect multiple areas, with the qualitative distortion of normal development, social interaction, of cognitive abilities, communication patterns and imaginative activity.

Personality Disorders

Personality disorders are difficult to define without an understanding of personality and personality assessment. We can describe personality disorders as a form of developmental disorder that particularly affects interpersonal relationships. So, the person's own inner thoughts, assessments and actions, as well as perception of external impressions.

Unlike more neurotic disorders, where one often finds an internal conflict, personality disorders are perceived to be developmental psychology rather than coping strategies over an undefined psychological deficiency condition, which may be unconscious, again created by insufficient external conditions or by external relationships unconsciously linked to childhood trauma. Although personality disorders he has a different cut than the typical neuroses, there is little doubt that in several personality disorders clear neurotic features are also found.

Personality disorders are often characterized by psychologically deeply rooted and rigid behavior patterns that persist over time. This means that the person responds in the same way in many personal and social situations without the ability to see whether behavior is appropriate or not. The behavior is adapted to the ego's attempt to appear flawless. At the same time, the person may act differently from different persons. Based on the other person's "utility and utility" in the daily mastery, one person may experience such individuals as completely rigid, while other people do not see this pattern at all because other people are not in any "struggle" with the one who suffering from a disorder. The sick individual himself seems to have a conscious or unconscious controlled behavior that is tailored to the utility of the present persons for this individual.

Psychopathy is a personality disorder. It is considered one of the most serious. Especially because of the character of the suffering and its ripple effects.

That is the way in which the character traits appear to be the pathological, not the trait itself. In other words, it is the quantitative size of the personality trait that determines the pathological level, not the trait itself. Ex.: All people lie, but psychopathic individuals lie about almost everything. All people use some form of manipulation in the daily, however, psychopathic individuals manipulate almost all the time. They not only manipulate others but can apparently "manipulate" themselves into believing that most things are going.

One of the better definitions of what a psychopath is defined by American psychologist Sullivan: "A psychopath is an individual who has wonderful ideas about what goes on, between people."

The trapped pattern of these traits testifies to the illnesses inability to adapt we find in the normal. It is also a paradox that psychopaths' attitude to life is the main cause of the fate that meets them.

Personality changes are unlike personality disorders, a condition that occurs in adulthood in previously normal individuals. The change occurs as a result of severe trauma or long-term stress. A personality disorder is also of a more original character, while a personality change occurs after an event and has thus not been present in the same way before.

It is well known that personality disorders occur together with other mental disorders such as depression and anxiety, which we call comorbidity. Few personality disruptions come into contact with the health service. No drugs have any direct effect on personality disorders, but on some troublesome symptoms such as. Depression, anxiety, difficulty sleeping and aggression. In patients with personality disorders, the tendency to depression begins early in life.

The incidence of personality disorders is high in depressed people. Shea et al (1987) describes that the incidence of personality disorders in depressed patients is between 37 and 87%. In inpatients, personality disorders in the dramatic group (borderline, histrionic, antisocial) are particularly common, whereas in outpatient patients, personality disorders in the anxious group are more common (avoidance, dependence, coercion). Shea and her co-workers examined outpatient patients with severe depressive disorder and found that 74% had personality disorder as well. Those with personality disorders in the dramatic group were heavily charged.

Scientists believe that it is possible that the more frequent and more chronic depression periods, at least in part, are a consequence of the personality disorder. "These patients may be emotionally more vulnerable, so they more easily respond to depression on life events and stresses". Depression seems more to follow from the person's development and interpersonal interaction. This becomes a vicious circle. The personality disorder causes depression, which in turn reinforces the personality disorder.

Personality disorders are defined by personality traits. The traits occur in the common population but are not as many or occur to a lesser extent. Personality disorders are thus only quantitative differences from normality. Professor Tollak B. Sirnes says the following: "By psychopathy, we understand a condition that is characterized by purely quantitative degeneration. "

"It is only when personality traits are non-flexible and non-adaptive and either lead to significant curtailment, in social functioning or work function, or to subjective suffering, that they constitute a personality disorder".

The tendency to develop some personality disorder is based on 30% inheritance (genetic), 10% common environment and the rest 60% on individual environmental factors.

Concepts

Scientists should show healthy skepticism in conclusions from data. This does not mean that researchers should be negative, but that researchers must always be on guard against alternative interpretations of observations and findings. A researcher always asks for the evidence that underlies specific conclusions, and whether other possible conclusions can be imagined: How can you conclude as you do? What other possible conclusions are available? Such skepticism is important in science. It is crucial for scientific advancements to eliminate possible but erroneous conclusions. This can only happen if research systematically questioned conclusions that researchers are launching. Scientists are also skeptical for another reason. Because cheating in research sometimes occurs, stringent requirements are set for documentation of the research result.

Let us take a closer look at some important concepts that we need to be aware of when we involve people with mental disorders. Likewise, it is important to know these concepts in order to reveal both the patients claims, but also the "conclusions" and the "understanding" that the people suffering from various disorders have.

Reliability

This is regarding the extent to which different investigators agree when they independently consider the same patient. If more researchers come to the same result in different surveys, the result can be said to be credible. Repeated tests give different testers the same result. Of course, it is assumed that the researchers involved have used scientifically recognized methods and the same methods. If one goes through the case again and does not reach the same result or finds that significant parts of the background material is omitted, the survey has poor realism.

Reliability means - consistency! If the same measurement is repeated several times and the same result is obtained each time, the target is relative. It is to be noted that these goals do not have to match reality. Here it is essential that different measurements of the same situation or object give the same result. Reliability does not say anything about the true value of the measurement. The idea of science is the highest possible reliability and the highest possible validity!

Validity

If a researcher keeps certain information outside of an evaluation, we will say that this has low validity. We have a low validity when the accuracy of the assessment is not much better than chance, and that one has not been able to specify the procedure for the assessment which means that no one can really verify such an assessment. An investigation based on untrue premises will thus have very low validity.

Validity is defined in the Oxford English Dictionary as follows:

"the quality of being well-founded on fact, or established on sound principles, and practically applicable to the case or circumstances, soundness and strength (of argument, proof, authority, etc.)"

Validity, example:

When we observe psychologically interesting conditions, such as aggression, helpfulness, or kindness, we interpret what we see. How do we know that the interpretation is correct? This is a question of validity. If you observe a person who gives a helping hand to another, you can reasonably interpret this as kindness or helpfulness.

But it's possible that you're wrong. For example, Freud believed that many actions that on the surface look like kindness or helpfulness are in fact expressions of underlying aggression. The person does the opposite of what his aggressive impulses suggest (reaction formation). Do you believe in Freud, the validity of the interpretation of friendly action can be wrong? Is it a friendly act or is it the opposite?

When it comes to psychopaths, this is to a great extent a topical issue. Their ability to manipulate is well known. An example may be a parent (psychopathic) who in a child custody case expresses an expert psychologist that "he / she hates lies and cheating!" If the expert does not register these lies, then he will interpret the validity of his statement as valid. On the other hand, if he reveals the lies, the statement from him will not be particularly valid! On the contrary, it is not just a direct lie, but at the same time there are several pathological defense mechanisms in use.

The lie can be seen as an expression of the underlying aggression she feels for her ex-husband. It would not be difficult to understand the consequences if the expert omits or does not have access to information that the lying lie! As we can see from the examples, failing validity can have serious consequences. This shows how important validity is in psychological science.

Validity has to do with durability, reliability. Are our descriptions of the impressions we receive good enough? Are our closures valid? The prerequisite for establishing sustainable knowledge is that it is possible in practice to distinguish between unsustainable and sustainable knowledge, between conclusions that are valid and conclusions that are not valid.

It becomes important to find out if conclusions are durable. How can we know that? A scientific conclusion is valid when a reasonable conclusion is formulated, and when alternative (reasonable) conclusions are excluded.

This means that correct conclusions are not valid until alternative conclusions are excluded!

Svartdal (writes in the book Psychology's research methods), the following:

"The fact that the researcher concludes that a given conclusion is valid is not a guarantee that the conclusion is correct. Science offers many examples that erroneous conclusions have been accepted as correct. But the likelihood is great that such errors are detected and corrected. Science is self-correcting. It means that even adopted truths are followed in the seams from time to time."

If data has satisfactory validity, it is much easier to draw good conclusions than if the validity is low. Research is entirely dependent on the data (premises) to be considered being valid. If data is not valid, they give a poor or distorted picture of what is to be considered.

Logic

Logic has a very important place in science and research. When we draw conclusions from observations (Induction) and when we divert implications from theories (Deduction) it is important that we know what we do. A conclusion is valid if it follows from the premises, it is logical!

Deduction

We have deductive logic, or deduction when a conclusion is derived from a theory or a well-established discovery. This is a better study method in cases where one has to deal with mentally ill patients. Deduction does not relate to what one immediately observes, but to well-founded truths that have been tested and found with a far greater degree of objective truth than, for example. by induction.

In deducing, we have a theory or hypothesis first, so we dedicate observation statements that we test. Unfortunately, many scientists today are not looking for the objective truth that emerges from falsifying their theories. Instead, they try to find evidence that supports their theory. The problem is that there can be an infinite number of findings that support a theory, but if one finds a discovery that does not support the theory, then it must be rejected. This is an indispensable scientific criterion, to which professionals are bound. The "professionals" who do not use such criteria can with good reason be called quasi-researchers! Many expert psychologists act this way today. They have a "theory" or assumption and are seeking evidence to confirm it. Everything that forces it is overlooked or omitted.

Induction

Inductive reassessment is based on individual cases and draws general conclusions based on these individual cases. One common factor to all forms of induction is that we adhere to something that is unknown and unseen. There is also a common feature of induction that the end is not necessarily valid. The conclusion does not follow logically from the premises. It is always possible in principle that the conclusion we draw is wrong. The danger lies in the generalization of an observation. In research, unlike daily life, there are clear limitations for what conclusions one can draw from a material. The fact that it is apparently easy to "see" a cause is not a criterion for being a proper cause. In the face of mentally ill individuals, it is often the case that they want us to believe what they want us to see through the use of examples. Therefore, through projective identification they try to make us not only believe but to be the way they want us to be. And they succeed many times.

We see trends, regularities and relationships in observations that are then generalized to cases that so far have not been observed. Such conclusions are vulnerable, as only an observation that does not match the end will falsify the conclusion! We thus divert a general truth from observed facts. This type of derivative is therefore very vulnerable in connection with mentally ill patients. Inductive logic when it comes to mentally ill patients is a contradiction of dimensions.

The falsification principle is important scientifically. The principle states that evidence supporting a hypothesis is less informative than evidence that falsifies a hypothesis. Why? Well, because affirmative evidence is consistent with a large number of hypotheses or theories, while falsifying evidence will rule out any hypotheses.

Not least, this is important for correcting for man's natural ability to "see what we want to see", that is, our preconceived notion. In matters related to psychopaths, this becomes very important. For health professionals who face a victim of a psychopath, it is easy to interpret the descriptions that are given as a normal conflict between two people. (See what you want to see, or what you tend to see) We do this based on an expectation that this is what we usually experience. Our cognitive form of what such situations apply to is often difficult to change.

Brief Psychotic Disorder

Psychopaths are masters of creating illusions as well as projecting their own mistakes and deficiencies onto the victim. The victim's frustrations are easy to misinterpret as aggression. The fact that the psychopath himself appears as a victim is classically described in much literature. It is therefore extremely important that in an assessment, where psychopathy is suspected, what one immediately experiences against information that indicates the opposite view. This is particularly important in situations where there are preconceived attitudes to situational images. In an expert report, the expert will have formed a view of the case. When that is done, is it important that the expert tries to falsify his or her vision? Is there anything that speaks to my "conclusion"? If there are 20 things that speak for and two that speak against, the two will be enough to allow the expert's opinion either to be rejected or corrected in the report. Otherwise, we have a report with elements that violate the conclusion of the report. It is always possible for such reports to find evidence that confirms a vision, rather than looking for evidence that claims a theory and does not find it, it is more reassuring than looking for evidence and omitting evidence that contradicts.

As an example, it can be mentioned how the psychologist in a child custody case failed to include all documents about the other party's psychic behavior. A deviant psychopathic, narcissistic behavior well documented many years back in time. The only thing the psychologist was interested in was finding information that substantiated one view in the matter. What supported the psychologist's subjective vision? The children in the case in question went from a safe, good life to being moved to the psychopathic persons care. This is when a healthy and well-functioning child ended up in ICU for treatment. Even after that, the psychologist refused to take over all the evidence hidden from court. There are many similar cases around the country I have documentation on. It is therefore important that professionals falsify their "hypotheses" in cases where these types of personalities are involved.

If the report believes a mother is best suited as a caregiver, the expert must, according to the principle of falsification, try to falsify this hypothesis. Perhaps there is information that mother is psychiatric abnormal! Or that she has lied about what she is telling, a lie that may have formed the basis of the hypocrite's hypothesis about who is best suited as a parent. Through falsification, such is revealed. There will always be arguments for a hypothesis, while it is enough to argue that the hypothesis must be rejected.

Assessment

Characterized by the fact that an assessment is made according to strict and well-defined rules, the advantage of actuarial assessment is many. Greater validity and reliability are some. In addition, the method is transparent, that is, the basis for the assessment that is made is clearly specified and thus available for verification by others. It weakens a professional work. It does not hold scientific goals.

Category VS. Dimensional

For the classification of psychopathy, there are two main methods to use. The categorical that clearly indicates either or. Either you are a psychopath, or you are not a psychopath. The second classification method is the dimensional. There are degrees of suffering and not necessarily something either. The PCL-R system is dimensional. It is divided into 40 points, and a limit of 30 points is set to diagnose psychopathy in research. This limit is approx. 25.

But what about the one who gets 24 points or 20 for that matter? The person can still be a terrible person. It is thus important that one does not blindly see a categorical understanding of the dimensional system. Those with 25 points are psychopaths, those with 24 are not!

Within research it may be important to set such limits, but in real life such categorical boundaries or cut-off have little meaning. There, the most important thing must be what people are exposed to through abuse and harassment from the psychopath. It doesn't help children much if their mother has 23 points and thus destroys the children emotionally. A categorical diagnosis cannot be made because it requires 25 points! It is therefore very important to look at the real consequences in the individual case and not to lock to a specific cutoff. For children it may be enough that the caregiver lacks empathy and is chronically lying. If other significant features are missing or weak, then the children are in an unsustainable care situation. This is important to be aware of, not least when it comes to psychopathy, which is a diagnosis that, with its taboo attachment, creates strong emotions.

Truth

In research context, this is a problematic term. No one has been aware of how the world really is. And when dealing with mentally ill patients, one should pay particular attention to this. Time and again it turns out that what you see and hear is not necessarily the truth or reality, but a manipulated situation. And most often that is the version a mentally ill patient wants to believe in. According to scientific practice, there is no absolute truth. On the other hand, one can talk about more or less the probability of something.

Validity

Validity is often used for logical conclusions. Are they valid or invalid? If logical conclusions are valid or do not depend on whether they follow from the premises. In some cases, such conclusions may be valid (they follow from the premises) but the content at the end may be incorrect. Likewise, it is important for validity that the premises are true.

High reliability says nothing about validity. Low Reliability does not necessarily mean low validity. We can say that diagnostic systems and checklists increase the reality. Research or studies with low validity or reality are not considered to have scientific validity, as the probability of the conclusions being wrong is great. Using open, recognized methods increases the reliability (that others come to the same answer). In order for the validity to be good too, the methods used must be the same. Thus, a result of a study will hardly achieve a high degree of validity unless the study is reliable and valid.

Problems in the Research

Suspicion of cheating or use of fabricated data occurs when researchers have reported a finding that others are unable to repeat using the same procedures. Psychologists and other professionals who go into examinations where psychopaths are included must be particularly observant that the premises they base on can actually be verified as true. Omitting background information or proving focus on a vision becomes equality as cheating. This is very serious as the result can often have catastrophic consequences. Good professionals are characterized by their research and work being transparent and containing all relevant information. A survey based on only parts of a relevant material is not in accordance with scientific standards.

Reactivity

Reactivity is present when the one being studied is affected by being studied. If a person's consciousness of being observed affects behavior, this is a threat that affects both validity (truth, reliability) and reactivity (credible, repeatability). Reality is affected if the observation method reduces the reliability (validity) of the information. Reaction formation is a typical example of reactivity.

The observed suppresses his aggression that would otherwise appear, so that the observer sees the opposite.

A mother observed by the child welfare service shows an apparently loving care for their children during the observation. An almost excessive caring ability appears. This is typical of psychopaths. What we see is signs of reactivity. In such cases, it is important to compare what is observed with other information.

In child custody cases where it is suspected that one of the parties presents psychopathic features, one should be aware of such mechanisms. Not only are the parents in a stressful situation, but they fear losing contact with their child. Some of the worst a person can experience. A person who, already at the outset (the psychopath) is fighting an inner psychological struggle to lure his or her more or less chaotic feelings, will then easily use different defense mechanisms to show off to the contrary a behavior they themselves believe is the best for them self. Such pressured situations are incredibly stressful for psychopaths. It appears by their use of a variety of defense mechanisms such as projection, reaction formation, denial, passive aggression, somatization / hypochondria, and the like.

Frode Svartdal writes the following about reactivity: "An obvious source of error in systematic observation is reactivity. The one observed is affected by being observed. "

Errors

It is difficult to treat information objectively. There are a number of sources of error in all forms of research that also emerge in psychology. Here is a list of some of them:

> 1. Data overload: It is limited to how much information we are able to process at one time.

2. First Printing: Early information is often given great weightage and forms are kept for interpretation of later information.

3. Availability of information: Information that is easily accessible often gets more attention than information that is difficult to access.

4. Confirming evidence: We tend to emphasize information that matches our expectations and ignores information that does not match expectations.

5. Internal consistency: Information that deviates from a pattern we have already attached to, often adds too little weight.

6. Data can often have varying degrees of reality: Some types of data are safe, others are uncertain. In the processing of complex information, we tend to regard all data as equally reliable.

7. Incomplete information: If we have missing or incomplete information about something, it is easy to underestimate the information we have.

8. Revision of hypotheses: When new information emerges, we tend to either overreact (revise the hypothesis too much) or be too conservative (revise the hypothesis too little).

9. Thought trend: When we draw a conclusion, we often have a tendency to compare with a thought average, even though this average is not known.

10. Trust in one's own judgment: When we conduct a review, we have excessive confidence in this assessment.

11. Coincidence: When we observe that two events occur simultaneously, we tend to interpret this as a correlation.

12. Inconsistency in data processing: When we go through a given set of data several times, it often happens that the conclusions of the data material are different from time to time.

In addition to the above-mentioned sources of error, there are significant sources of error associated with human perception. Human perception and interpretation of the impressions one experiences. Two people can experience an impression completely different based on gender differences, cultural differences, political differences, etc.

Within psychology, it is said that the whole is more of a sum of the parts. Likewise, it can be questioned whether one really sees what one thinks one sees. There is every reason to be aware that many see what they want to see and that must be distinguished from an objective view. In contact with psychopathic individuals, it is important to be aware of such conditions.

Stress Model

I choose to bring this here as it is important for the vision that begins to emerge in research that the interaction between biological and environmental factors is of great importance for the formation of personality disorders. This model assumes that behavior is a result of both genetic, biological and psychological factors including life experiences. According to this model, personality disorders are formed as a result of interaction between some vulnerability factors, or pre disposability and a triggering event in the environment. It can be a trauma or a very invasive experience in early childhood, but also before the baby is born.

Psychotic disorders include a large number of mental disorders that share common symptoms such as hallucinations, delusions or disorganized thinking. The intensity of these symptoms and their duration varies greatly from one disorder to another.

I am fortunate to meet several people with a long-term psychotic disorder and we would like many to be as sane as they are.

They are perfectly aware of their disease and control their medication themselves.

Others, of course, others are functionally affected, but this happens in psychotic disorders and in life in general.

With this introduction I want to start where it usually ends; saying that it is possible to live well, be happy, work and at the same time deal with a psychotic disorder.

What Is A Psychotic Disorder?

More than in the singular, we should talk about psychotic disorders in the plural, because there are several.

Psychotic disorders are a spectrum of mental disorders ranging from milder disorders, such as schizotypal personality disorder, to schizophrenia, its most complex end.

Does it amaze you to see a personality disorder classified as a psychotic disorder? Well it appears in the latest version of one of the manuals that follow the mental health professionals to establish a diagnosis, the Diagnostic and Statistical Manual of Mental Disorders in its fifth edition (DSM V).

And in fact, psychosis as a symptom is present in many mental alterations, beyond those that accept the category of psychotic disorders. For example, in bipolar disorder psychotic symptoms can be experienced without this being a psychotic disorder itself.

But this is not enough that I have told you to understand what a psychotic disorder is, right? Because these alterations are best understood through their symptoms.

Psychotic disorder symptoms

According to the DSM V that I mentioned before, there are five symptoms that define a psychotic disorder, these are:

Delirious Ideas

The person has wrong beliefs, which do not change despite clearly demonstrating that they are wrong.

A very common delusion is that the person believes that they want to harm him, be it his neighbors, caregivers or an institution.

I know the case of an elderly patient who considers that her caretaker is stealing her pension, a delirium that is repeated very often.

Hallucinations

Hallucinations are unreal perceptions of stimuli that have not really occurred, but the person experiences it as a real experience.

The most common are auditory hallucinations; for example, the cases in which a person thinks they hear someone giving them orders, and visual hallucinations, in which the person believes they see things that are not really there.

Disorganized thinking

It is detected primarily through language, noting that the person jumps from one topic to another without any apparent connection, even if it remains in the same central theme, the ideas that manifest have no natural link.

It can also happen that his speech has no meaning for those who listen to him, with individual words without connection to each other.

Disorganized behavior

Disorganized thinking is especially noticeable in language, disorganized behavior is particularly reflected in motor activity.

We can see the person agitated, with movements that do not have a specific purpose (very often I see a person with schizophrenia that does not stop walking constantly) or on the contrary, totally rigid and without apparent response to any external stimulus (a symptom known as catatonia).

Negative symptoms

Negative symptoms are the least known and perhaps the most suffering in psychotic disorders.

They are not new symptoms, but rather the affectation of activities and processes present in everyone.

We refer to symptoms such as diminished emotional expression, which are manifested in an extra verbal expression "flat", lacking facial expression and also in the lack of intonation during speech.

Another frequent negative symptom is the difficulty to initiate activities on their own initiative, which often causes others to accuse the patient of "not wanting to do anything" and not to "make an effort".

Causes of psychotic disorders

As with most mental illnesses, the exact causes of a psychotic disorder are not identified.

It is considered that they have a strong genetic base and that the relatives of people with a psychotic disorder have a higher risk of developing the disease (you may have references of families in which schizophrenia has marked several members of different generations), but in most of cases, genetics alone is not enough to cause the disorder.

Then there is talk that a genetic predisposition can be precipitated by traumatic or stressful life events, such as the death of a loved one, the breaking of a relationship or the beginning of a new period of studies.

The precipitating factor does not necessarily have to be a vital event of great depth, it can also act as such the exposure to certain substances. For example, it is not uncommon to hear testimonies from people who had their first psychotic episode after having tried marijuana.

In addition to the above, in recent years the idea that schizophrenia, in particular, may be a disorder of brain development that has its roots before birth or in childhood has gained strength.

Here, too, there is the question of what can cause the atypical development of the brain. The answers are very broad: genetics, prenatal factors such as exposure of the mother to toxic substances, malnutrition or infections.

Schizotypal Disorder

Also known as schizotypal personality disorder, it can be considered a mild form of these disorders.

People with schizotypal disorder have difficulty establishing interpersonal relationships and are often considered eccentric or peculiar.

The disorder is often accompanied by delusions, not as severe as those seen in schizophrenia, but sufficient to interfere with their relationships with others.

Delirious ideas can make the person interpret that the gestures of those around him are directed to her, when in reality it is not like that, or that she can lead her to believe that she has special powers and abilities.

Schizophreniform Disorder

This disorder represents an intermediate point between brief psychotic disorder and schizophrenia.

A schizophreniform disorder is diagnosed when the person manifests at least two of the symptoms that characterize the psychotic disorders and that we mentioned at the beginning, that is:

- Delusional ideas
- Hallucinations
- Disorganized thinking
- Disorganized behavior
- Negative symptoms

But and this is important, the symptoms that the person experiences must include, at least, one of those first three symptoms.

In addition, it must be taken into account that the schizophreniform disorder manifests itself for at least one month, but for less than six months, this characteristic distinguishes it from schizophrenia.

People who remain with a diagnosis of schizophreniform disorder do not usually experience great impairments of their functional abilities, however, it must be taken into account that up to two thirds of the individuals who initially receive this diagnosis, are finally diagnosed with schizophrenia or schizoaffective disorder.

Schizophrenia

The term Schizophrenia was coined by the Swiss psychiatrist Eugene Bleuler in 1908 and derives from the Greek Skhizein (Excision) and Phen (Mind). It refers to a split of the basic functions of the personality, which, according to this psychiatrist, is the cause of the unusual behaviors of those affected by schizophrenia. The popularization of this conception generated the erroneous idea that every person diagnosed with schizophrenia has double or multiple personalities. Concepcion popularized in movies and novels as already commented before.

Symptoms of Schizophrenia

The heterogeneity in the symptoms that the person suffering from Schizophrenia manifests is commonly grouped in three important blocks: Positive Symptoms, Disorganized Symptoms, and Negative Symptoms.

Positive symptoms

They represent the most obvious symptoms of a state of psychosis so that their mere presence is already indicative that the person is in a psychotic state. However, it is essential to consider several criteria to discriminate if the positive symptom responds to a brief psychotic episode, to schizophrenia or another type of mental disorder. Positive symptoms of Schizophrenia, Delusions, and Hallucinations are considered.

Delusions

Fixed beliefs that the person keeps even in the presence of evidence that refutes or is against him. Delusions can be classified according to the theme that stands out. Among the most recognized we have:

- Persecutory Delusions: a Fixed belief that one will be harmed, persecuted, harassed, etc.

- Referential Delusions: A fixed belief that gestures, comments, signals from the environment, etc. are directed to one when, in fact, it is not.

- Delusions of Greatness: the Fixed belief that the person possesses wealth, fame, or exceptional qualities.

- Erotomanic Delusions: the Fixed and erroneous belief that another person is in love with him or her.

- Somatic Delusions: Fixed and erroneous belief regarding their poor health or malfunction of their organs.

- Delusions Nihilist: Erroneous belief that a great catastrophe is looming.

Hallucinations

They are perceptions that take place without the presence of an external stimulus. These perceptions are considered by the person who suffers with the force and impact of a normal perception and is not subject to voluntary control. It can manifest itself in any sensory modality. However, it is the auditory hallucination that is more frequent in these patients and consists of the experimentation of voices (known or unknown) that are perceived as different from the own thought.

Disorganized Symptoms

They represent erratic behaviors that affect speech, motor behavior, and emotional reactions and include Disrupted Speech or Speech and Disorganized or Catatonic Behavior.

Disorganized Speech

This symptom is considered extremely serious if it hinders communication in a meaningful way. Through Speech or

Disorganized Speech, we can infer that equally the thoughts of the person diagnosed with Schizophrenia, are disorganized. This Disorganized Discourse is expressed through Decay or Lax Associations: The person changes from one topic to another. Tangentiality: the responses of the affected person may be indirectly related to the question or not. Incoherence: Commonly called "Word Salad" where the language is practically incomprehensible.

Disorganized Behavior (Including Catatonia)

This symptom in the schizophrenic patient could hinder the execution of daily activities. Among the expressions of this symptom we have: Catatonia: It is a marked decrease in reactivity to the environment and ranges from resistance to follow instructions (Negativism) to the adoption of a rigid, inadequate or extravagant posture with the total absence of verbal or motor responses (Mutism and Stupor). Catatonic Excitation: Excessive motor activity without purpose or apparent cause.

This group can also include repeated, stereotyped movements, fixed gazes, grimaces, mutism, and echolalia.

Negative symptoms

It refers to the absence or insufficiency of normal behavior. The negative symptoms that stand out most in schizophrenia are: Decreased Emotion Expression: The person with schizophrenia does not accompany or give emotional emphasis to his speech due to a decrease in the manifestation of his emotions through his facial expressions, eye contact, intonation in speech, movements of the head, hand and face. The subject presents a decrease in their activities by their own initiatives and motivated by a purpose, so it is possible to keep hours in one place and without showing any interest in participating in any social or employment activity.

Diagnostic Criteria of Schizophrenia

For the effective identification of Schizophrenia, the Diagnostic and Statistical Manual of Mental Disorders, better known as DSM-5, has established a set of criteria to consider:

A.- Two or more of the following symptoms must be present, for a minimum period of one month (less if it was treated successfully) and at least one of the symptoms presented must correspond to symptom 1, 2 or 3.

Delusions

Hallucinations

Disorganized speech

Very disorganized or catatonic behavior.

Negative symptoms

B.- There is a deterioration in functioning in one or more major areas (work, personal relationships, personal care) or performance below expected if it begins in childhood or adolescence.

C.- During the minimum period of six (6) months should persist the negative signs or two or more of the symptoms of Criterion A in a less accentuated way (Example, strange beliefs, unusual perceptual experiences). In these six (6) months must also be present, at least one month (less if treated successfully) of any of the symptoms of active phase of Criterion A.

D.- The Schizoaffective disorder and the Depressive or Bipolar disorder with psychotic characteristics have been ruled out.

E.- The disorder is not attributed to the physiological effects of a substance or other medical condition.

F.- If there is a history of a spectrum disorder of autism or a communication disorder of onset in childhood, the additional diagnosis of schizophrenia is only made if the delusions or hallucinations are notable, in addition to the other symptoms required for schizophrenia , they are also present for a minimum of one month (or less if successfully treated).

Levels of Gravity of Symptoms of Psychosis

The Diagnostic and Statistical Manual of Mental Disorders or DSM 5, established new parameters to indicate the level of severity of psychotic symptoms, disabling the previous classification that existed of the Schizophrenia types. It is to indicate that in the previous version, the DSM IV TR, Schizophrenia was classified into five Subtypes:

- Paranoid schizophrenia.
- Disorganized schizophrenia.
- Catatonic schizophrenia.
- Undifferentiated schizophrenia.
- Residual schizophrenia.

The Subtypes of Schizophrenia are no longer identified, but this is determined according to the predominant symptom at the time of the evaluation and act as specifiers that allow to further detail the diagnosis. This change in the DSM 5, allows to assess the level of severity of the psychotic symptom in other mental disorders where they can also be manifested, since many of these are not exclusive of Schizophrenia.

The classification of the Gravity Levels of the Symptoms of Psychosis in the DSM 5 includes other domains such as Cognitive Alteration, Depression and Mania.

Clinical and Psychoanalytical description of Schizophrenia

Schizophrenia is one of the mental disorders that generates the most negative impact on the person and their family circle, since in general, these people are not aware of illness and directly influences their level of social functioning (Labor, academic, family). Their level of chronicity increases as the years go by if the disease is not treated in time and this level is even higher, if it is detected in adolescence or childhood. Certainly, the lower the level of schizophrenia and the greater control of the disease, the greater the options for the subject to maintain a high level of social functioning.

Schizophrenia tends to start in men at the beginning of their twenties and in women from the second half of the twenties. The onset may be abrupt and insidious, but most have a slow and gradual evolution of symptoms.

A subject who presents Persecutory Delusions (Paranoia), will stand out for being very suspicious in the establishment of personal and social relationships, will formulate complex conspiracy theories against him and will act defensively before other people since he considers that others will want to hurt him , damage it or betray it. This attitude implies by default, that those around him, family members, study or work colleagues, decide to depart from these subjects because they are constantly accused by the affected party of conspiring against him. The person who manifests delusional ideas or hallucinations, maintains affectivity or behavior in a normal way. It is in the residual phase (after the manifestation of the positive symptom) that the negative symptom could manifest itself, thus generating the deterioration of affectivity in the subject.

There is a risk of suicide, especially in schizophrenic persons with paranoid delusions or with very marked auditory hallucinations, who in turn maintain constant problems of interpersonal relationships and serious impairments in social functions.

The person diagnosed with Schizophrenia may present somatic concerns that are not necessarily delusional, eating disturbances, untidy and incongruous physical appearance, inappropriate sexual behavior, inappropriate affection such as laughing in the absence of an appropriate stimulus.

From the psychoanalytic point of view, Sigmund Freud, the father of Psychoanalysis, postulated that the Neurosis is expressed by a conflict between the Ego and the It, while Psychosis arises from a conflict between the Ego and the Outer World. In this way, the subject with schizophrenia what he does is a denial of reality to later remodel it. This happens because the ego has not developed normally, so its operation has been very altered and must resort to very primitive defense mechanisms that require deforming reality to balance. This unsatisfactory development of the ego can be the product of early traumas, affective deficiencies during early childhood, etc.

In the Schizoid-Paranoid Position, through the libidinal and aggressive impulses towards the external object (Mother's Chest), the child creates the image of the Good Object and the Bad Object. Both objects, when introjected, constitute the first core of the ego and the superego. If in these first four months, the aggressive impulses give rise to very intense paranoid anxieties, the fantasies of persecutory objects that will hinder the introjection of good objects and the development of a core of healthy ego and superego will predominate.

Therefore, the I will massively and pathologically produce the corresponding Schizoid Dissociation and Projective and Interjective Identification Mechanisms and the I will not be able to advance or adequately elaborate the Depressive Position, period between the fourth month of life until the first year. of life, where the child would diminish his anxiety of being attacked by the Bad Objects since he will have managed to integrate or merge the Good Objects and the Bad Objects into a Total Object that will possess both qualities, as well as diminish the use of the Schizoid Defense Mechanisms and the fear of losing the Good Object will arise, giving as a step, the development of other more evolved Defense Mechanisms.

If the advance to the Depressive Position is not done in a harmonious way, this will reinforce the Schizoid-Paranoid Position, as well as the use of Schizoid Defense Mechanisms widely used by people diagnosed with Schizophrenia as Excision, Dissociation, Projective Identification and Interjective Identification and will lay the foundations for the emergence of Schizophrenia.

Causes and Risk Factors of Schizophrenia

Genetic Factors: Genes explain between 63% and 85% of the vulnerability to suffering from schizophrenia. A relationship has been found with chromosomes 6, 8, 9 and 20, as well as the long arm of chromosome 22. The risk of suffering from schizophrenia increases if the person has a family member with Schizophrenia or Schizotypal Personality Disorder.

Home and Prenatal Factors: Mother over 39 years old, anemia, previous abortions, prolonged labor, multiple births, calcification of the placenta, respiratory problems of the newborn, very sensitive or irritable baby, high level of Cortisol (stress hormone).

Neurological factors: There is a high relationship between the neurotransmitter of Dopamine and the positive symptoms of psychosis: delusions and hallucinations. The greater the presence of this neurotransmitter in the brain, the greater the chance of experiencing these symptoms. Other risk factors to consider are: Epilepsy, seizure, stroke, tumors, multiple sclerosis, head injury.

Social Factors: While there is a genetic and neurological predisposition of certain people, which makes them vulnerable to suffer Schizophrenia, the truth is that it arises if environmental and social conditions provide the right means. In this we can cite: Dysfunctionality in the mother-child relationship when this was a neonate or was in its first months of birth, family environment or highly stressful work which generates high loads of anxiety to the subject, experience of some current trauma that triggers his vulnerability to schizophrenia: death of a relative, emigration to another country, etc.

Narcotics: It has been proven that the consumption of amphetamines and cocaine increases the probability of presenting paranoia since these stimulate the level of dopamine in the brain. Cannabis (Marijuana) is related to auditory hallucinations, in addition to negatively affecting short-term memory, diminishing attention, judgment and other cognitive functions.

Differential Factors of Schizophrenia

Major Depressive Disorder or Bipolar Disorder with psychotic or catatonic features. The main distinguishing factor is the temporal relationship between the alteration of mood and psychosis and the level of severity of depressive and manic symptoms. If delusions and hallucinations occur exclusively during the period of the major depressive or manic episode, then the diagnosis will be a Depressive or Bipolar Episode with psychotic features.

Schizoaffective disorder. This diagnosis requires that a major depressive or manic episode occurs concurrently with the symptoms of the active phase and that mood symptoms are present for most of the total duration of the active periods.

Schizophrenia Disorder and Brief Psychotic Disorder. The differential factor is time. In Schizophrenia Disorder the alteration is present for less than 6 months, while in Schizophrenia the negative symptoms last at least 6 months. In Brief Psychotic Disorder, symptoms occur for at least one day but less than one month.

Delirious Disorder. It is distinguished by the absence of other symptoms characteristic of Schizophrenia such as: prominent auditory or visual hallucinations, disorganized speech, very disorganized or catatonic behavior, negative symptoms.

Schizotypal Personality Disorder. These symptoms are below the threshold (intensity level) and are associated with persistent personality traits.

Posttraumatic Stress Disorder. It requires the presence of a traumatic event and the symptoms of reliving or reacting to this event to justify its hypervigilance that can become paranoid.

Autistic Spectrum Disorder or Communication Disorders. They are distinguished by deficits in social interaction, with restricted and repetitive behaviors and by other cognitive and communication deficits.

Treatments of Schizophrenia

The complexity of the Schizophrenia deserves that its approach is pooled between different health professionals, such as psychologists, psychiatrists, nurses and social workers, as well as between different mechanisms of approach. It has been proven that the effectiveness of these treatments is more effective if they are implemented together, if only one is implemented to the exclusion of the others.

Pharmacological. Pharmacological treatment is fundamental to achieve the recovery of the schizophrenic patient, especially if it is in the active phase of the positive or disorganized symptoms of Schizophrenia. Among these drugs we can highlight:

Antipsychotics: They allow us to cope with the positive symptoms of schizophrenia, such as Delusions and Hallucinations, by acting on the decrease of dopamine, a neurotransmitter in the brain which is related to these symptoms. This treatment usually remains several months after the remission of the active phase of the positive symptom at lower doses, to avoid a possible relapse. Among the antipsychotic drugs we can include Haldol, Risperidone, Olanzapine and Clozapine.

Antidepressants: This group of drugs allows us to treat the depression that arises in these patients, and even allows us to address the negative symptoms of schizophrenia and acute and subacute extrapyramidal symptoms.

Benzodiazepines: Effective for the treatment of acute catatonic reactions, they also act in cases of agitation or insomnia. They are used as a complementary treatment to antipsychotic drugs, especially during the acute phase of Schizophrenia.

An important aspect to emphasize of the pharmacological treatment, is that the patients with diagnosis of Schizophrenia, eventually do not continue the treatment due mainly to the secondary effects that these could cause. Some of these side effects are: lightheadedness, blurred vision, dry mouth, extrapyramidal symptoms, etc. However, with the emergence of Atypical or Second-Generation Antipsychotics, many of these effects, if any, are attenuated.

Psychoanalysis or Psychodynamic Therapy. Firstly, we must identify the phase of schizophrenia that the subject is experiencing and if he is in a condition for psychotherapy. Many times, in active phases of schizophrenia, high doses of antipsychotic drugs are required to control the positive or disorganized symptoms of the disease, however, these could disturb or hinder psychotherapy. If this is the case, it is advisable to offer supportive psychotherapy until the subject is able to start or continue psychotherapy. Once initiated, the therapist should:

- Establish contact with the psychotic thought of the subject so that he feels safe and understood.

- Establish continuity between reality and hallucinations and delusions, as well as between its history of past life and its present symptomatology. It is important to make a good anamnesis, in which the exact moment in which the psychotic symptoms began is determined, since this will allow us to help the patient with their conflicts and anxieties.

- Provide security through understanding and interpretation and acting as the patient's Auxiliary in terms of proof of reality and judgment, in order to balance aspects of life that the patient cannot do for himself.

- Structure the patient's life in such a way as to create the bearable conditions of coexistence that allow him to cope with the psychotic episode and alleviate, at least temporarily, the tension generated by the illness. Example, consider moving to a country house for a while if your current environment is highly stressful and does not provide the minimum conditions for mental recovery, reducing the level of work or other situations that are generating high emotional or physical demands.

- Availability on the part of the therapist to attend, if necessary, to the patient in cases of emergency.

- Introduce the significant others in the patient's life as parents, partners, children, close friends to maintain communication with the subject and establish a support network.

- Consider Brief Hospitalization if necessary, in order to balance the patient's situation, however, it will be essential to continue psychotherapy, even within the mental care center, so that the patient does not feel that he has been abandoned and this affects even more his state of mind.

Group Therapy: This therapy allows the schizophrenic patient, a space in which he can express himself and share with people who suffer from the same disease. In general, these group sessions are supervised by the psychologist and allow him to observe his patients in the context of social interaction. The group sessions allow us to face the Social Stigma towards people with a diagnosis of mental illness, diminishing, in turn, the development of self-stigma and the emergence of possible depressive episodes.

Psychoeducation: It allows the development of social and cognitive aspects of the person affected by Schizophrenia through role plays in which social relations stand out, the knowledge of the disease and its implications, the development of personal hygiene habits, emotional intelligence, social skills and above all, adherence to treatment. This last point is fundamental, since many patients diagnosed with schizophrenia abandon pharmacological treatment due to the presence of some side effects.

Family Therapy: Given the impact that schizophrenia generates in the family environment of the schizophrenic patient, it is essential that the psychologist influences positively in order to provide them with the support tools to support the day to day with their family member, as well as to identify the intrafamily dynamics that could affect a possible relapse and the possible cases of depression or anxiety among the members when confronting this disease.

Schizophrenia usually strikes young people at the end of their twenties or early thirties.

It is diagnosed when two or more of the psychotic symptoms that we have been seeing (being at least one of them hallucinations, delusions or disorganized thinking) manifests itself during most of the time during at least one month.

In addition, the person with schizophrenia maintain significant alterations for six or more months, including negative symptoms such as apathy and flat affect, which significantly affect functioning in daily life.

The evolution of schizophrenia is not the same in all patients. In a limited number of cases the recovery can be given, in another percentage, around 20%, the patients evolve favorably and with the appropriate medication they manage to lead an independent life.

Another group, the most nourished, will need support throughout their lives because they will have recurring periods of crisis in which the psychotic symptoms will appear, followed by remissions, phases in which there are no positive symptoms such as hallucinations or delusions, but symptoms negative as cognitive deficits.

Schizoaffective Disorder

This disorder manifests itself in symptoms very similar to those of schizophrenia, that is, with delusions, hallucinations, disorganized thinking and behavior, as well as negative symptoms.

The great distinction with schizophrenia is the presence of a significant affective alteration, be it a major depression or mania.

Schizoaffective disorders are very controversial, with some researchers suggesting that it is a variant of schizophrenia where cognitive disorders predominate and others considering that it is an affective disorder where psychotic symptoms do not completely remit.

In addition to these psychotic disorders that we have mentioned here, perhaps the most classic and representative of the entire spectrum of schizophrenia, there are others such as psychotic disorder induced by substances or psychotic disorder due to another medical condition that also has a significant incidence in the population.

How is a psychotic disorder treated?

There are two fundamental lines of treatment, pharmacological and non-pharmacological.

Both are indispensable, because while the drugs used for the treatment of psychosis, the so-called antipsychotics, help to control the positive symptomatology, most do not have a significant effect on the negative symptoms.

There are two types of antipsychotics, typical and atypical. Both have a similar effectiveness in the control of symptoms, but differ in the safety profile, with atypical being associated with fewer side effects.

Likewise, it is important to bear in mind that the search for the most effective treatment for each person can take a long time of trial and error. Patience no longer give up.

Finally, insist on the importance of non-pharmacological interventions, those that can offer professionals in psychology, occupational therapy and social educators.

Their work is key to the approach of negative symptoms and to insert the person into the social fabric.

Remember that the goal is not only to control hallucinations or delusions, the goal is also to build a life full of meaning and satisfaction.

Schizophrenia is a mental disorder that presents a set of psychotic symptoms very different from each other. In this way, we can observe a person who covers his head with a layer of aluminum so that the extraterrestrials or the government does not inquire his thoughts, another subject who says hear voices or see people who have died and communicate with him and even, people that we can observe with a lost look and with a sparse or scarce communication with the other, without the slightest expression. These people possibly suffer from schizophrenia, a major mental disorder characterized by cognitive and emotional dysfunctions.

Schizophrenia is perhaps, along with Psychopathy, one of the mental disorders that has had the most representation in our culture, either in numerous films, TV series and / or books, standing out in most of these representations, due to its distortions in the thought (Hallucinations and Delusions) and aggressive behaviors against other people, even reaching mass murder. However, for sure, not all these characterizations of people with diagnoses of Schizophrenia adequately describe the symptoms of this disease, generating much confusion in society and above all, raising the level of rejection and fear towards these people in an unfounded manner.

Narcissistic Personality Disorder

Here, I want to elaborate on the term narcissism, as it is a very central sea for most personality disorders and not least psychopathy. Without a fundamental understanding of the concept of narcissism, it is impossible to understand the disorders.

The concept is about egocentrism, morbid self-absorbed, pathological grandiose, a false self-image and is almost a prerequisite for most other personality disorders. As far as I know, there are no personality disorders where the person also does not have significant narcissistic features. There is comprehensive literature on this term. Initially, the term appears to be made visible through psychoanalytic, psychodynamic theory, and object-relational theory. But the concept is also strongly promoted in development theory, but in a non-pathological context.

Important development theorists such as Jean Piaget (1926, 1977) and Bowlby et al. point to the infant's natural narcissistic desires in the first years of life. While this behavior at this stage of development is a normal aspect of personality, the child grows from it as it accommodates the environment. The child's cognitive form is adapted to new impressions and expectations from the environment. There are many indications that problems caused by the child from close caregivers through an authoritarian, negligent upbringing or over-protective upbringing do not allow the child to acquire and grow this narcissistic behavior, but instead is caught in an endless attempt to meet the needs of the early narcissism is meant to cover for the infant, but as abnormal upbringing and experiences from the surroundings of early childhood did not give rise to. It may seem as though the child's pathological narcissism is a posterior one of the important caregivers' lack of understanding that the child is an independent individual. The child has acted as a narcissistic supply for his caregivers, where either the caregivers dumped their own defects or where the caregivers in a naive belief that they protect the child have thought that the child should not suffer the same fate as they themselves suffered. This with the result that the child has been overprotected, and thus has not learned the "hard school of life." When the child is to stand on his or her own legs, the protection is gone, and the child is seeking where the protection was. Namely, with the different caregivers! It becomes a vicious circle, where the young mother seeks her own mother to confirm her own life. The result is false self-esteem they both try to live up to. The older mother in a spacer from her parents and the younger mother in a desperate quest for the glorifying image her mother has imprinted on her.

Problems at this stage of development are what one is assuming today is part of the explanation that some people develop a foundation of extreme vulnerability and loss experiences that merge so closely into the person that it becomes a permanent part of the personality. Personality disorders are also some of the most difficult to treat in humans and disorders such as psychopathy, etc. there is also no effective treatment for. One can at best treat some of the symptoms we see around psychopaths.

Daffodil

Daffodils or Narcissus poeticus, have got their name from the gravest myth of Narcissus who fell in love with his own reflection and admired himself until he died. Socrates called narcissus for "the chaplet of the infernal goods." Homer, who, despite finding the flower's discretion, believed it could be the cause of apathy, insanity, and death! The name comes from the Greek Nakao (= numb)!

Narcissism seems to exist in two basic forms. An introvert type and the more familiar extrovert type. The first describes the retracted narcissistic personality, while the other is the more outgoing type. The outgoing type appears to be the one described at first glance in the DSM. This outrageous, often frenzied type is described in terms such as;

One who does not care, thick skin, egocentric, grandiose, arrogant, who requires attention but who do not care or have feelings for others. In other words, empathy-less individuals.

People who are easy to get sympathetic towards are the more introverted type that appears far more self-confident, does not like sticking out, but exhibits the same tendencies as an extrovert. It is not just about clothes, but also how they want others to see them. They love fine cars, extremely neat clothes, and are sometimes paranoid about cleanliness. The description "I want I want, but do not get it" is so striking for these individuals. They often splurge on people around them. Be it social security or partners. Their style of parasitic life is well described in literature. They are described as watchful, thin-skinned, vulnerable, very sensitive to signals from others. They are described as self-destructive, vulnerable, and dissociative.

The latter plays on his "poor me" attitude when the resistance seems too powerful and compassionate from the environment that does not see through its very complex and advanced manipulations. Lies and impotency are not uncommon. Logical shortcomings, as we find in mentally ill patients, are also common.

One way to describe or distinguish between normal and narcissists is that the normal person reflects his himself, is flexible and can withstand ambient criticism of themselves. The ego is self-critical, strong, and can withstand challenges without any widespread use of unproven defense mechanisms. Capacity for accommodation and correction of existing cognitive form is present. The person adapts to the world and not the other way around. We can say that "healthy narcissism" or a normal person can be characterized as having full access to their true self.

The narcissist, on the other hand, reflects his false self for fear of revealing his actual weak self, is rigid, and does not tolerate the environmental criticism towards him. Typically, they react with insults when subjected to criticism. For them, criticism is tied up with shame. Their ego is weak, and their superego is strict, at least when the narcissist talks about others than himself. The demands of others' moral actions are high but do not reflect their own respect for the same moral demands. Statements like "I hate lies and cheating" apply to others, while the narcissist himself can lie, so he or she believes it herself!

The use of pathological defense mechanisms can be extensive. Keeping everything that seems uncomfortable to them from a distance requires a comprehensive mental apparatus that must be broadcasting 24 hours a day. They are not only exposed to threats from the environment but also from their own imagination and dreams. The ability to accommodate is not very well developed; the surroundings can adapt to the narcissist and not the other way around. It is also in their grandiose infallible nature that they obviously do not need to change. A demand for change gives them the feeling that something else is more perfect than them and is, of course, for them, a contradiction of dimensions.

The vulnerable sensitive was described as defensive, hypersensitive, anxious, and socially restrained whose personal relationships were marked by their ability to enjoy themselves, foolishly, and demanding things to happen in their own way. High scores on grandiose exhibitionists display a stable behavior pattern of humility, exhibitionism, and the propensity to enjoy themselves, and disrespect for others. The most prominent difference between the two main types seems to be anxiety and pessimism, the inability to stand out, giving up on jobs and relationships and great vulnerability to life trauma. The vulnerable-sensitive type is very complex, multi-faceted, and that many of their characteristics are very difficult to measure through self-reporting or through observations.

Other professionals have attempted to put different names on these two types of narcissists.

Kets de Vries and Miller (1985) described three types of narcissists in their investigation:

1. Reactive narcissists
2. Self-Deceptive Narcissists
3. Constructive narcissists

Here the first two are considered more pathological than the latter.

Bursten 1986 in Essential papers on Narcissism, describes 4 different types of narcissists. They were:

1. The Craving
2. The Paranoid
3. The Manipulative
4. The Phallic

At the same time, he writes that he has never seen a pure profile but that the different profiles have some overlapping features. Empirical studies have shown that this Type 1 narcissist has valid research support. Other narcissistic types span the whole scale, and some show both extremes in some individuals.

Sam Vaknin talks about "Healthy narcissism" and "Pathological narcissism," but makes it quite clear that the term "Healthy narcissism" is a template-based term and that the two concepts have no connection. "Pathological narcissism" describes a dysfunctional, immature and self-connected person with a substitute self (the false self). The self-sense of the sick narcissist deviates completely from the impression of the surroundings. The narcissist has no self-esteem and no ego function. Thus, the superego also gets greater power over the person's behavior. There are no normal brakes. As a spectacle player, a narcissist without an "audience" proves to be just an empty shell with inner negative forces.

Pathological narcissism is the result of superficiality associated individuals with the displacement of obscuring memories and experiences from early childhood. We talk about emotional feelings such as pain, envy, anger, and humility. These are emotions the child was once exposed to, and it never came across. Likewise, they are pathological liars. To conceal its interior, the lie becomes part of the game to preserve the false mask outward.

Importantly, depression is extremely common in narcissists. The "depression" one finds with some narcissists are of a rather special nature. One does not always find the typical down-to-earth pessimism (with the exception that they sit alone with a doctor and have social security to live on). One finds an outgoing personality that can start court cases, manipulate, run an active game, where the mask is adapted to the purpose. The inexperienced psychologists have more than once overlooked the narcissist diagnosis and believed it was a common depression they faced. In child custody cases, this ends tragically for children where they are sent to the "depressed" / narcissistic mother rather than the healthy father. The "depressed" then has more than once proved to be a pure narcissist.

In the book Malignant Self Love, Sam Vaknin describes a narcissist type which he calls Inverted Narcissist! He writes that this type of narcissist was previously described as a Covert narcissist. However, there seem to be some differences between these two. An inverted narcissistic is closely related to the DSM Dependent Personality Disorder. In fact, according to Sam Vaknin, a criterion for being called Inverted Narcissist. However, this basic type seems to be similar to the child of a narcissist, who then, in a customary manner, almost learned to become the parent's narcissistic supply and who himself uses the parent as his narcissistic supply. This link to Dependent Personality Disorder is very interesting. It is a typical feature of the introverted narcissist that one finds a high degree of comorbidity between dependent personality disorder, but also of avoidant personality disorder, and the introverted narcissistic. It can sometimes cause confusion if you do not know both of the diagnostic lists. They seem so intertwined that there is every reason to assume a certain relationship between them.

David Kelly describes another type of narcissist that he calls Compensatory Narcissistic Personality.

Dependent Personality Mistake

Depending on the personality disorder as described both in the ICD-10 and the DSM, you can see the close links between narcissism and dependence on others. This is a disturbance, whose features are, to a large extent, found in the narcissist. Paul Kelly (1998) writes the following:

"The Diagnostic and Statistical Manual of Mental Disorders, Fourth Edition describes Dependent Personality Disorder as a pervasive and excessive need to be taken care of that leads to submissive and clinging behavior and fears of separation, beginning by early adulthood and present in a variety of contexts, as indicated by five (or more) of the following:

- has difficulty making everyday decisions without an excessive amount of advice and reassurance from others;

- needs others to assume responsibility for most major areas of his or her life;

- has difficulty expressing disagreement with others because of fear of loss of support or approval;

- has difficulty initiating projects or doing things on his or her own (because of a lack of self-confidence in judgment or abilities rather than a lack of motivation or energy);

- goes to excessive lengths to obtain nurturance and support from others to the point of volunteering to do things that are unpleasant;

- feels uncomfortable or helpless when alone because of exaggerated fears of being unable to care for himself or herself;

- urgently seeks another relationship as a source of care and support when a close relationship ends;

- is unrealistically preoccupied with fears of being left to take care of himself or herself.

Mc Williams (1994) states there are two postures to the narcissist. One in which he will convince himself that he has attained his unrealistic dreams (the grandiose posture) and one in which he is a failure (the depressive posture).

The narcissist is shallow, and although he may offer gestures of self-sacrifice, these are for the sake of appearance. At the core of the narcissist is a sense of entitlement. He believes that his presumption of superiority is proof enough, and he should not have to prove its existence. He thinks that if he wants something that he should get it no matter the cost to others.

Akhtar (1992) warns that the narcissist has difficulty comprehending or accepting the incest taboo. Sexual behavior is possible with his children if he does not see them as separate individuals who are not there for his gratification.

The narcissist is self-absorbed, emotionally immature, and lacks empathy for others. He is unable to establish intimacy and may actually deny his need for personal relationships. He is adept at the use of defense mechanisms and can easily justify his self-centeredness and his inconsiderate treatment of others.

The false self of the narcissist hides his inner emptiness. He hides his feelings of being unwanted, unlovable, inferior, and not belonging. It would be easy to feel sorry for the narcissist; however, the presentation of his false self, which he presents to the world repels others and does not evoke other's sympathy. The narcissist receives from those he comes in contact with what he fears most -- rejection.

Most narcissists are, as it stands today, men. However, there are many indications that there is a change of pattern, and as societal structures change towards the egocentric individual, the inequalities are diminishing between the sexes. It is clearly seen that women carry out precisely the same harmful, ego-fixed activities as what we associate with narcissistic men.

Narcissistic Personality Disorder is one of several personality disorders in a family that fall in the DSM called Cluster B. Other members of this family are an antisocial personality disorder, table line, and histrionic disorder.

Narcissistic Personality Disorder is often diagnosed with other disorders of this family as well as disturbances from depression and anxiety disorders. Often, the lack of diagnosis of this disturbing disorder is due to more of a defect in the database layer of the person than the features are omitted in the person's behavior. Lack of foundation and knowledge among professionals is another serious threat to narcissist victims, be it children or adults.

The two main types of narcissism, the extrovert and the more introverted can be difficult to disclose. Especially the introvert, who is well-validated through research, but who is not that well described in diagnostic systems. It can, therefore, easily be confused with more common depression. Only a more in-depth analysis will diagnose this. Professionals have, in many cases, been allowed to be manipulated by such introvert narcissists to believe that they have depression, which can trigger whole or partial social security.

Although narcissism has been described by Ellis (18xx), it is only about 1970-80 that various theorists have seriously debated it, and then primarily from the psychodynamic perspective. Freud was the first to describe it in 1914 in the form of pathological narcissism. Other important contributors are Klein, Horney, Kohut, Kernberg, Millon, Roningstam, Gunderson, Hare.

Narcissism has its origins in early childhood and academic literature over many decades shows it is linked to the caregivers' influence, both positively and negatively. It is often linked to trauma and negligence-induced withdrawal patterns. Too much reputation is just as bad a foundation as too little care. It is the extremes that often in combinations with a weak mother and possibly alcoholic father give the child an early pathological self-image.

Narcissists usually divert their narcissistic supply from intelligence and academic efforts. In such cases, the narcissistic supply is derived from its physical appearance, fitness, sexual behavior, and reassurance it brings. In addition, as previously mentioned, there are two main types, either the outgoing, classic or the more introverted, enclosed type.

Pathological Narcissism

From a psychoanalytic point of view, we are all narcissists from an infant age. We are like little gods and omnipotent. This is sometimes referred to as primary narcissism.

As the awareness of the environment increases, the feeling of invulnerability diminishes. We experience our first disappointments and trauma. If we do not get food when we want, we do not need the attention we require to relate to others than the primary cares we were used to. Our primary narcissism is sharpened more in step with reality. For some children, however, this does not happen. They are treated as if they were the mother's / father's extended body part, and never get detached and connect their normal development mentally to a growing person. Instead of new impulses being accommodated in our mental forms of the environment, they are assimilated into our cognitive reality. In other words, the world must adapt to us and not the other way around.

Of course, it does not take long before our inner real self understands that this creates problems. Thus, we compensate with a pathological false self exterior so that for the environment it will look as if we are well-adapted. Just as well-suited as what we thought, we were like an infant in our mother's embrace. This, of course, goes wrong in the end. It all becomes a constant struggle against the disclosure of the actual self for the environment. This struggle requires enormous mental resources to maintain. It will struggle in your interior, and you end up with depression and worse. Not only for 2-3 month but chronic. The lack of self-understanding of problems means that narcissists do not seek help for anything other than their symptoms, e.g., depression when it becomes too difficult or influences too much in family life, or whether one can use their symptoms to their own gain by spamming on others, which is common among them.

It is when the idea of the narcissist (the false) meets the reality that the problems come to the surface. The narcissistic rage is hellish, comes as lightning from clear skies and can often be linked to feelings and situations of jealousy, humiliation, etc. Fluctuations between devaluation and idealization of the environment do not contribute to reducing this problem.

Bitter disappointment is often the basis of the adult narcissist. Healthy adults accept their condition; the narcissist does not. They have no concept of their limitations in everyday life. Everyday life for them is like the one they experienced in their omnipotent time as an infant. In adulthood, where they have to take care of themselves, this becomes difficult. Disappointments, losses, and criticism become impossible for the narcissist to handle. They become displaced, projected, and divided by the legitimate part of their reality. This causes both internal and external problems.

Different Understanding Of Pathological Narcissism

Various psychodynamic and psychoanalytic models incorporate Libido (the driving force) along with Thanatos (the death force) into Freud's theories. Along with other theorists such as Horney and her cultural context, Sullivan's interpersonal relationships, as well as neurobiological and neuro-chemical forces, form the basis for a deeper understanding of the narcissism spiritual aspects. The object relation theorists have made significant contributions in this respect and are well among the most prevalent explanatory models today.

Common to all these different theories is that development is a continuous process of inner and outer forces in an infinite interaction. Obstacles to development are explained in various ways, and in some, psychopathology becomes an outcome where development has encountered significant challenges. This, in combination with the individual's special equipment genetically and molecularly, gives rise to various manifestations in the form of different personality disorders. Some worse than the others. Growth occurs at all costs, developments do not stop but may go into the wrong, ugly pathological sidings. The final personality may be abnormal, but it has overcome difficult obstacles on the road. Regardless of how many "reefs are in the sea," it's strange it goes as well as it does so many times.

Diagnostic Criteria For Autism And Autism Spectrum Disorder (ASD)

The conception of autism has changed significantly in recent years, thanks to the advance in its research. The latest version of the international classification of major mental disorders, the Diagnostic and Statistical Manual of Mental Disorders-5 (DSM-5), recognizes these developments and includes autism within neurodevelopmental disorders, moving away from the old conceptualization of Disorder Generalized Development (TGD). In contrast, the other international classification of mental disorders, the International Statistical Classification of Diseases and Related Health Problems-10 (ICE-10), maintains the old classification. Neurodevelopmental disorders are a group of disorders that have their origin in the gestation period. They are characterized by deficiencies in development that produce limitations in specific areas or global limitations at a personal, social, academic, work, etc. level.

In addition, autism is now called Autistic Spectrum Disorders (ASD), since it recognizes the autistic symptomatology common to all individuals in a wide range of phenotypes. It is for this reason that the subtypes of autism disappear (Rett Syndrome, Asperger's Syndrome, Childhood Disintegrative Disorder, Generalized Developmental Disorder Not Otherwise Specified).

In this classification, it is considered that the fundamental characteristics of autism are: a development of social interaction and communication, clearly abnormal or deficient, and a very restricted repertoire of activities and interests.

Below are the diagnostic criteria for Autism Spectrum Disorder (ASD) according to the DSM-5 (APA, 2013).

A. Persistent deficiencies in communication and social interaction in various contexts, manifested by the following, currently or by background

A.1 Deficiencies in socio-emotional reciprocity; for example:

- Abnormal social approach,
- Failure in normal conversation in both directions,
- A decrease in shared interests, emotions or affections,

A.2 Deficiencies in nonverbal communicative behaviors used in social interaction; for example:

- Less integrated verbal and nonverbal communication,
- Abnormality in eye contact and body language,
- Deficiencies in the understanding and use of gestures,
- Total lack of facial expression and nonverbal communication

A.3 Deficits in the development, maintenance, and understanding of relationships; for example:

- Difficulty adjusting behavior to different social contexts,
- Difficulties in sharing the imaginative game or to make friends,
- Absence of interest in other people

B. Restrictive and repetitive patterns of behavior, interests or activities manifested in two or more of the following points, currently or by background (the examples are illustrative but not exhaustive)

B.1 Movements, use of objects or stereotyped or repetitive speech; for example:

- Simple motor stereotypes,
- Alignment of toys,
- Change of place of objects,

- Echolalia,
- idiosyncratic phrases

B.2 Insistence on monotony, excessive inflexibility to routines, or ritualized patterns of verbal and nonverbal behavior; for example:

- High anguish at small changes,
- Difficulties with transitions,
- Rigid thinking patterns,
- Greeting rituals,
- Need always to follow the same route or eat the same foods every day

B.3 Very restrictive and fixed interests that are abnormal in their intensity and focuses of interest; for example:

- Strong link or high concern towards unusual objects,
- Overly circumscribed and persevering interests

B.4 Hyper or hyperactivity to sensory stimuli or unusual interest in sensory aspects of the environment; for example:

- Apparent indifference to pain/temperature,
- Adverse response to specific sounds and textures,
- Smelling or touching objects excessively,
- Visual fascination with lights or movements

C. Symptoms have to manifest themselves in the early development period. However, they may not be fully disclosed until social demands exceed their limited capabilities. Strategies may mask these symptoms learned later in life.

D. Symptoms cause significant clinical deterioration in the social, work, or other important areas for normal functioning.

E. Alterations are not better explained by intellectual disability or by an overall developmental delay.

The DSM-5 (Diagnostic and Statistical Manual of Mental Disorders), considers that the fundamental characteristics of autism are: a development of social interaction and communication clearly abnormal or deficient and a very restricted repertoire of activities and interests.

Intellectual Disability (ID) and ASD are frequently linked. To make a diagnosis of ASD and ID with comfort, social communication must be below what was expected at a general level of development.

Persons previously diagnosed, according to the DSM-IV, of autistic disorder, Asperger's or generalized developmental disorder not specified, will currently be diagnosed with ASD.

Likewise, people with notable deficiencies in social communication, but who do not meet criteria for the diagnosis of ASD , have to be evaluated to diagnose a new disorder that has been defined by the DSM-5 called "communication disorder (pragmatic) social " The main difference with an ASD is that in the social communication disorder the diagnostic criterion B is not met, so that there are no restrictive and repetitive patterns of behavior, interests or activities

And in addition to the diagnostic criteria, you must specify whether:

It is accompanied or not by intellectual disability,

It is accompanied or not by language deterioration,

It is associated with a medical or genetic condition, or a known environmental factor,

It is related to another disorder of mental neurodevelopment or behavior, with catatonia,

The level of severity must also be specified:

Level 1: need help

Level 2: need remarkable help

Level 3: you need very exceptional help

If we analyze the content of these diagnostic criteria, we observe that, independently of the two fundamental symptoms, a criterion referring to the symptomatologic onset is included (C), so that only the Autism Spectrum Disorder can be diagnosed if criteria A and B are manifested during early childhood. The reason for the inclusion of this temporal criterion is to be able to differentiate between ASD, which, by definition, appears very early, from the disintegrative disorder of childhood, which manifests itself after a period of apparent normality not less than two years after age.

Neurodevelopmental Disorders

There are various types of neurodevelopmental disorders (symptoms and causes)

These mental alterations can significantly harm the well-being of the little ones if no treatment is given.

When we think of disorders or mental problems, it is easy for problems such as depression, bipolar disorder, schizophrenia, or phobias to come to our mind. Here we will review what the types of neurodevelopmental disorders and the category to which they belong are.

Neurodevelopmental disorders are the set of mental difficulties that have their origin in a non-neurotypical development of the brain or the presence of alterations or injuries in its maturation.

They have their origin in early childhood or during the development process, and it is usually possible to detect the first symptoms early.

The alterations caused by these disorders generate difficulties of varying intensity in the process of adaptation and social participation and in the performance of basic activities for survival. The activity of the subject is limited or altered with respect to what would be usual in other subjects with the same age and conditions.

Intellectual Disabilities

Intellectual disability is considered one of the neurodevelopmental disorders, due to deficiencies or difficulties of intellectual functions and adaptive behavior in its conceptual, practical or social, which have as a consequence a possible limitation of the functioning of the subject in one or more vital areas unless they have specific support.

Also included in this group is the global developmental delay, which is diagnosed when it is not possible to assess the severity of the disorder in children under five years of age, although it is observed that it does not meet the expected developmental milestones. This diagnosis is provisional.

Definition of Intellectual Disability

Limitations on present functioning should be considered in the context of typical community environments of peers in age and culture.

A valid evaluation must take into account cultural and linguistic diversity, as well as differences in communication and sensory, motor, and behavioral aspects.

In a person, limitations usually coexist with capabilities.

An important purpose of the description of limitations is the development of a profile of support needs.

If appropriate personalized supports are maintained over a long period, the functioning in the life of the person with intellectual disability will generally improve.

This approach considers disability as the adjustment between the person's capacities and the context in which it operates and the necessary supports.

Intellectual functioning is related to the following dimensions:

Intellectual skills

Adaptive behavior (conceptual, social and practical)

Participation, interactions, and social roles

Health (physical health, mental health, etiology)

Context (environments and culture)

The terminology proposed by the AAIDD is as follows:

Mild intellectual disability

Moderate intellectual disability

Serious intellectual disability

Deep intellectual disability / multi-disability

Intellectual disability of unspecified severity

Intellectual Development Disorder

The Diagnostic and Statistical Manual of Mental Disorders DSM-5 of the APA in its 5th edition (2015) defines INTELLECTUAL DISABILITY (intellectual development disorder) within the NEURODESARROLLO DISORDERS, a group of conditions whose onset is in the period of development and that includes limitations of the intellectual functioning as well as of the adaptive behavior in the conceptual, social and practical domains.

Classification

The DSM-5 (2015) proposes a classification of the intellectual development disorder according to the severity measured according to the adaptive functioning since this is what determines the level of support required.

Mild intellectual disability.

It is included in the same the students whose score in CI, without reaching 55 - 50, is below 75 - 70 (about two standard deviations below the average, with an error of measurement of approximately 5 points).

About this upper limit section, in the DSM-5 it is indicated that mild disability could be diagnosed with an IQ between 70 and 75 if there is a significant deficit in adaptive behavior, but not when it does not exist.

Students with a mild intellectual disability account for approximately 85% of cases of intellectual disability. In general, they tend to present slight sensorial and/or motor deficits, acquire social and communicative skills in the early childhood education stage, and acquire the basic instrumental learning in the primary education stage.

Moderate intellectual disability.

It includes students whose IQ score is in the IC range between 55 - 50 and 40 - 35. The adaptive behavior of these students is often affected in all areas of development. They account for around 10% of the entire population with intellectual disabilities. Students with this type of disability usually develop communication skills during the first years of childhood and, during schooling, may acquire partial basic instrumental learning. They usually learn to move autonomously in familiar places, attend to their personal care with some supervision, and benefit from social skills training.

Serious Intellectual Disability

It includes students whose IQ measurement is between 35 - 40 and 20 - 25 and accounts for 3-4% of the total intellectual disability. Acquisitions of language in the first years are usually scarce, and throughout schooling, they can learn to speak or use some sign of alternative communication. Adaptive behavior is very affected in all areas of development, but the learning of elementary personal care skills is possible.

Deep Intellectual Disability / Multi-Disability

The majority of these students present an identified neurological alteration that explains this disability, the confluence with others, and the great diversity that occurs within the group. For this reason, one of the areas of priority attention is physical health. The IQ measurement of these students is below 20-25 and represents 1-2% of the total intellectual disability. They usually present a limited level of consciousness and emotional development, no or little communicative intentionality, absence of speech, and serious motor difficulties. The level of autonomy, if it exists, is minimal. The casuistry supposes a continuum that includes from students "bedridden," with the absence of corporal control, to students who acquire very late some basic patterns of motor development.

Communication Disorders

The communication disorders are those disorders of neurodevelopment in which the subject is not able to communicate properly or learn to do so despite having sufficient mental abilities to do so.

Within this group of disorders, we find the language disorder, the phonological disorder, the pragmatic communication disorder or stuttering or speech fluency disorder of childhood onset.

Language Disorder

Changes in the classification of language development disorders

The development of language is one of the most important neuroevolutionary aspects. It is how children begin to communicate with their immediate surroundings - the family - and the nursery mates. Their cognitive and emotional development may be compromised depending on the quality of their implementation ("language is the food of intelligence"), although not all difficulties are equally decisive. Many of the difficulties encountered have a genetic component, and most of them are due to obstetric-perinatal or unknown causes.

In the development of verbal communication, we find several basic elements: pronunciation, production/expression, compression, and pragmatics. Throughout history, language disorders have been classified according to the anomalies found in one or several of these elements and taking into account the cerebral bases that encode them. In this post, I will not talk about stuttering because I consider it different in terms of etiopathogenesis and evolution.

Pronunciation Disorder

It refers to the anomalous pronunciation of the words (especially those that contain locked syllables) without medical abnormalities that justify it (the cleft palate, the orofacial dyspraxia, and the lingual frenulum or ankyloglossia are the most frequent). When we do not find any medical cause that explains them, we say they are functional. When there is a medical cause, they are called organic. Normally, functional ones resolve quite well with logopedic intervention.

Both the DSM 5 and the DSM IV call it a phonological disorder. Contrary to the following disorders, the phonological disorder is better defined clinically in the DSM 5 than in the DSM - IV. Both versions specify that it is a disorder of phonological production, which must produce a significant degree of interference in social communication, in academic or work performance. The DSM 5 specifies that its presentation occurs in the early stages of development. Both include as exclusion criteria any medical condition that can explain it.

Disorder of the Production / Expression of Language

This disorder disappears from the DSM 5 that is included in the category Language Disorder. In the DSM IV, it was defined as the presence of a very limited language, with errors in the tenses, difficulties in the memorization of words or the elaboration of sentences that due to their length and/or complexity are appropriate for the age. It should cause interference in academic or work performance and social communication.

The diagnosis was discarded, as such, if there was a medical cause or mental retardation to explain it.

Disorder of Language Comprehension

In the DSM - IV it is included in the category T Mixed Language of the Receptive-Expressive Language. Likewise, this category disappears in the DSM 5 and is included in Language Disorder.

The symptoms of the mixed disorder included those of the expressive disorder, in addition to the presence of difficulties in understanding the words, phrases, or specific types of words. Likewise, their interference must be significant in school performance, work, and social communication.

As in all the previous situations, the diagnosis itself is discarded when there is a medical cause or mental retardation that explains it and must be reflected in axis III.

Therefore, in the DSM 5 disappear as diagnostic categories, both the expressive language disorder and the mixed disorder of receptive-expressive language. As a first observation, we point out that if from a clinical-therapeutic point of view, the classification of the DSM IV was a reductionist one, in DSM 5, it is even more accentuated.

Disorder of Social Communication (Pragmatic)

DSM 5 introduces this new category that was necessary for several reasons. The first is that many patients with a prior disorder of language compression (a category that at the same time eliminates in this version) can evolve into a pragmatic communication disorder. The second refers to the fact that many patients who were previously diagnosed with Asperger's syndrome or high functioning autism are better reflected clinically in this category than in the autistic spectrum disorder.

Pragmatic Disorder of Communication

Neither DSM IV nor version 5, developed the diagnostic categories on language development disorders so that they can be useful for the clinic and therapeutic intervention (logopedic) due to its reductionism. They are only useful for studies of prevalence that inquire about this problem of development in a general way and thinking more about the need for resources than in the clinic.

Developmental dysphasia, especially all problems of language compression, are diluted in the category "Language disorder," losing all its specificity, so important for a logopedic intervention, and the prognostic evaluation.

By including errors in writing in the category of "language disorders," it hinders the diagnosis of reading-writing disorders, forcing us to perform double diagnosis in some cases.

I consider the new category "communication disorder (pragmatic)" very positive since it is a clinical reality that will serve for future investigations, both entomopathogenic and therapeutic applications.

The classification proposed in the DSM 5 does not facilitate the entomopathogenic investigations in the other categories since it has constructed a tailor that includes them, and that reduces their specificity. This lack of specificity produces errors in the research designs (selection bias) that are statistically insurmountable.

The Fluidity Disorder Beginning In Childhood (Stuttering)

A. Alterations in normal speech fluency and timing that are inappropriate for the individual's age and language skills persist over time and are characterized by the frequent and noticeable appearance of one (or more) of the following factors:

1. Repetition of sounds and syllables.

2. Prolongation of consonant and vowel sounds.

3. Fragmented words (e.g., pauses in the middle of a word).

4. Audible or silent block (speech pauses, full or empty).

5. Circumlocute (substitution of words to avoid problematic words).

6. Words produced with an excess of physical tension.

7. Repetition of complete monosyllabic words (e.g., "I-I-I-I see it").

B. The disturbance causes anxiety when speaking or limitations in effective communication, social participation, academic or work performance individually or in any combination.

C. The onset of symptoms occurs in the early stages of the development period. (Note: Later onset cases are diagnosed as adult-onset fluidity disorder.)

D. The disturbance cannot be attributed to a motor or sensitive speech deficit, dysfluency associated with neurological damage (e.g., stroke, tumor, trauma) or other medical condition and is not better explained by another mental disorder.

Attention Deficit Hyperactivity Disorder

Another of the most well-known neurodevelopmental disorders, ADHD, is a disorder characterized by the presence of typical symptoms of intent. These can include difficulty maintaining attention, commission of errors due to lack of it, high distraction, non-completion of tasks, loss and forgetting of objects and activities, mental absence, and/or hyperactivity (talks excessively, motor restlessness, have difficulties remaining seated or waiting for their turn, interrupts other people's activities, etc.)

Symptoms of intention may predominate, hyperactivity symptoms may occur, or a mixed presentation may occur.

It is also possible to find cases in which there are no cases of hyperactivity but only of intention, which is now known as attention deficit disorder or ADD.

Specific Learning Disorder

A specific learning disorder is understood as one in which the subject manifests difficulties in the acquisition and use of academic skills, such as reading, writing, and mathematics.

The individual has difficulties when it comes to reading, interpreting, and using language (he has problems, for example, with grammar and spelling) and/or mathematical concepts. These difficulties are beyond what is expected for someone of the age and intellectual capacity of the subjects, interfering in their academic activity.

Motor Disorders

Another of the major groups of neurodevelopmental disorders are the motors, in which there are difficulties in aspects related to movement such as coordination or involuntary movements occur.

Within these disorders, we find the disorder of the development of coordination, stereotyped movements, and tic disorders. In this last group, we find the Tourette disorder, along with the persistent motor or vocal tics and transient tics.

Other Specified Attention-Deficit / Hyperactivity Disorder

This label is used in those disorders linked to neurodevelopmental disorders that cause an affectation of the subject in some or some vital areas, but that do not meet the diagnostic criteria of any of the previous groups of disorders.

For example, those disorders linked to substance use by the mother during pregnancy, or in those cases in which there is not enough information available to classify the disorder in question.

Developmental Coordination Disorder

From childhood, we acquire information about how to perform a certain task unconsciously and through experience.

This information is stored and consolidated in the implicit procedural memory to be recovered when we face the same task again.

But what happens when there is a deficit in this automation process? What happens is that important problems appear to acquire perceptual-motor habits and cognitive strategies that are basic for the child's development in their daily life.

What is the disorder of the development of coordination?

The Development Coordination Disorder (TDC) is a chronic and prevalent condition of neurodevelopment that causes a significant impact on the child's ability to learn and to manage with ease, in addition to their school activities, those that belong to their daily lives.

It is characterized by deterioration in motor coordination and cognitive and psychosocial skills. In the beginning, it derives in subtle difficulties to participate successfully in the tasks that arise during the first years of life. But with time, and if not addressed properly, has a very problematic impact affecting multiple aspects.

The main concerns of families tend to be around the secondary consequences of lack of motor coordination. These include an increased risk of childhood depression and anxiety, the onset of obesity, and diminished self-esteem.

It is also considered a global learning disorder due to a delay in the automation of information acquisition procedures, hindering a successful academic performance. It affects around 5-6% of children of school age, so it is advisable to start with the treatment as soon as possible to minimize the impact that these difficulties have on the performance of the youngest children.

Children with this disorder have significant limitations in their ability to plan and control motor.

Associated problems

As a consequence, problems appear in multiple processes, among which are:

- Reduction in the speed of processing information.
- Problems in the ability to generate beneficial strategies to achieve objectives.
- Deficit of control of the representation of actions.
- Problems to maintain attention.

All these, at the school level, are often reflected in difficulty to automate reading, writing or calculation, which in turn affects many other activities

Characteristics of the Development Disorder of Coordination

The main characteristics are the disorder of motor coordination, school learning, and social relations.

Throughout the study of this disorder have been used various names that refer to very similar characteristics: a specific disorder of psychomotor development, dyspraxia of development, DAMP (attention deficit, motor control, and perception), right hemisphere syndrome and nonverbal learning disorder. In 2009, the investigations of Narbona, Crespo-Eguílaz, and Magallón oriented this disorder under the name of Procedural Learning Disorder (TAP). However, the diagnostic guidelines DSM-5 and CIE-11 (of international use and recent revision) recognize this set of symptoms as a disorder of the development of coordination.

Clinical Criteria for Diagnosis

According to the DSM-5, the following clinical criteria must be met for diagnosis:

A. The acquisition and execution of motor coordination skills are substantially below expected for the chronological age of the individual and the opportunities for learning and use of skills. Difficulties are manifested as clumsiness (e.g., dropping or hitting objects), as well as slowness and poor precision in the execution of motor skills (e.g., picking up objects, using scissors or cutlery, calligraphy, riding a bicycle, or participating in sports).

B. Deficits in motor skills of criterion A interfere significantly and persistently in activities of daily living as expected for chronological age (e.g., self-care) and influence academic / school productivity, work activities, of leisure and game.

C. The onset of symptoms is in the early period of development.

D. Deficiencies in motor skills are not better explained by intellectual disability (intellectual development disorder) or visual impairments, and cannot be attributed to a neurological condition that alters movement (e.g., cerebral palsy, muscular dystrophy)., degenerative disorder).

Stereotyped Movement Disorder

The essential characteristic of stereotyped movement disorder is a repetitive motor behavior, which usually seems impulsive and is not functional. This motor behavior interferes with normal activities or gives rise to self-inflicted bodily injuries significant enough to require medical treatment (or this would occur if no protective measures were taken). If there is mental retardation, stereotyped, or self-injurious behavior is serious enough to become a therapeutic goal.

This behavior is better explained as a compulsion (as in obsessive-compulsive disorder), a tic (as in tic disorders), and a stereotype that is part of a generalized developmental disorder or hair pulling (as in trichotillomania). Nor is the behavior due to the direct physiological effects of a substance or to a medical disease. Motor behaviors must persist for at least four weeks (Criterion F). Stereotyped movements can include shaking hands, swaying, playing with hands, tapping with fingers, turning objects, head-butting, biting, pricking one's skin or body orifices, or hitting different parts of one's body.

Sometimes the subject uses an object to perform these behaviors. The behaviors in question can cause permanent and disabling injuries, which sometimes endanger the life of the subject. For example, headings or blunt blows can cause cuts, hemorrhages, infections, retinal detachments, and blindness. The clinician can specify self-injurious behavior if the behavior causes bodily harm that requires specific treatment (or that could cause bodily harm if protective measures are not used).

Symptoms and Associated Disorders

The subject may resort to methods of self-containment (e.g., keeping hands under the sweater, in pants or pockets) to try to control self-injurious behaviors. When self-containment interferes, behaviors are resumed. If the behaviors are extreme or repulsive to other people, psychosocial complications may arise due to the exclusion suffered by the subject regarding certain social and community activities. The disorder of stereotyped movements appears frequently associated with mental retardation. The more serious the delay, the greater the risk of self-injurious behavior.

This disorder can also appear associated with severe sensory deficits (blindness and deafness) and may be more frequent in institutional settings, where the subject receives insufficient stimulation. Self-injurious behaviors appear in some medical conditions associated with mental retardation (e.g., Fragile X syndrome, Lange syndrome, and especially Lesch-Nyhan syndrome, which is characterized by severe self-bleeding).

Laboratory Findings

If there are self-injurious behaviors, the laboratory data will reflect its nature and severity (e.g., anemia due to chronic blood loss due to self-inflicted rectal bleeding).

Signs of chronic tissue damage may be observed (e.g., bruises, bite marks, cuts, scratches, skin infections, rectal fissures, foreign bodies in the body orifices, visual disturbances due to ocular emptying or traumatic cataract, and fractures due to bone deformations). In less severe cases, there may be a chronic irritation of the skin or calluses due to bites, punctures, scratches, or salivary secretion. Symptoms dependent on age and sex Self-injurious behaviors occur in individuals of any age. There are indications that head butts are more prevalent in males (in a ratio of approximately 3: 1) and self-sores are in women.

Prevalence

There is very little information about the prevalence of stereotyped movement disorder. Estimates of the prevalence of self-injurious behaviors in subjects with mental retardation vary from 2 to 3% in children and adolescents living in the community and approximately 25% in adults with severe or profound mental retardation who live in institutions. Course There is no typical age of onset or a pattern of onset due to stereotyped movement disorder. This initiation may follow a stressful environmental event. In nonverbal subjects with severe mental retardation, stereotyped movements may be caused by a painful medical illness (e.g., an infection of the middle ear that results in head butts).

Stereotyped movements tend to be maximum in adolescence, and from that moment on, they can gradually decline. However, especially in subjects with severe or profound mental retardation, movements may persist for years. The goal of these behaviors changes frequently (e.g., a person may incur hand-biting, disappear this behavior, and then start banging his head). Differential diagnosis Stereotyped movements can be associated with mental retardation, especially in subjects located in non-stimulating environments.

The disorder of stereotyped movements should only be diagnosed in subjects whose stereotyped or self-injurious behavior is serious enough to constitute a therapeutic goal. Repetitive, stereotyped movements are a feature of pervasive developmental disorders. Stereotypic movement disorder is not diagnosed if the stereotypes are better explained by the presence of a generalized developmental disorder. The compulsions of obsessive-compulsive disorder are usually more complex and ritualistic and are performed in response to an obsession or following rules that must be rigidly applied.

It is relatively simple to differentiate complex movements characteristic of stereotyped movement disorder from simple tics (e.g., blinking), but differential diagnosis with complex motor tics is less easy. In general, stereotyped movements seem to be more motivated and intentional, while tics have a more involuntary quality and are not rhythmic.

By definition, in trichotillomania, repetitive behavior is limited to hair tractions. Self-induced lesions of stereotyped movement disorder should be distinguished from the factitious disorder with a predominance of physical signs and symptoms, where the motivation for self-injury is to assume the role of the sick. Self-mutilation associated with certain psychotic disorders and personality disorders is premeditated, complex and sporadic, and has a meaning for the subject within the context of the underlying serious mental disorder (e.g., it is the result of delusional thinking).

Involuntary movements associated with neurological diseases (as in Huntington's disease) usually follow a typical pattern, the signs and symptoms of the neurological disorder in question being present. Self-stimulating behaviors of young children typical of their level of development (e.g., thumb sucking, rolling, and nodding) are usually very limited and rarely cause injuries that require treatment. Self-stimulating behaviors in individuals with sensory deficits (e.g., blindness) do not usually cause dysfunction or self-injury.

Criteria For The Diagnosis Of Stereotyped Movement Disorder

Repetitive motor behavior, which seems impulsive, and non-functional (e.g., shaking or shaking hands, balancing the body, head-butting, nibbling objects, self-injuring, pricking the skin or holes) bodily, hitting one's body).

The behavior interferes with normal activities or leads to self-inflicted bodily injuries that require medical treatment (or that would cause an injury if preventive measures were not taken).

If there is mental retardation, the stereotyped or self-injurious behavior is of sufficient severity to constitute a therapeutic objective.

Behavior is not better explained by a compulsion (as in obsessive-compulsive disorder), a tic (as in tic disorder), a stereotype that is part of a generalized developmental disorder or hair pulling (as in trichotillomania).

The behavior is not due to the direct physiological effects of a substance or a medical illness.

The behavior persists for four weeks or more.

Diagnosis Of Tic Disorders

Tics are sudden spasms, movements, or sounds that are made repetitively. People who have tics cannot control them voluntarily. For example, it may be that a person with a motor tic flashes again and again, without stopping, or that a person with a vocal tic emits grunts involuntarily.

Tic disorders are differentiated by the type of tic that it is present (motor or vocal, or a combination of both) and for the duration of the symptoms. People with TS have both types of tics, motors, and vowels, and have had symptoms for at least one year. People with persistent motor or vocal tic disorders have motor or vocal tics and have suffered the symptoms for at least one year. People with a transient tic disorder may have motor or vocal tics, or both, but have presented symptoms for less than one year.

Below we present the diagnostic criteria in a summarized manner. Please keep in mind that they are here only for you to report and that they should not be used to self-diagnose. If you have concerns about any of the listed symptoms, you should consult with a trained health care provider experienced in the diagnosis and treatment of tic disorders.

Tourette's Disorder

For a person to receive a Tourette's Disorder diagnosis, they must meet the following criteria:

Having two or more motor tics (for example, blinking and shrugging shoulders) and at least one vocal tic (for example, humming, clearing the throat or shouting a word or a phrase), although it is possible that not all occur at the same time.

Have had tics for at least one year. Tics can occur many times a day (usually in attacks), almost every day, or from time to time.

Have tics that have started before age 18.

Have symptoms that are not due to the use of medications or other drugs or another condition (for example, seizures, Huntington's disease, or post-viral encephalitis).

Persistent (Chronic) Motor Or Vocal Tic Disorder

For a person to receive a diagnosis of persistent tic disorder, they must meet the following criteria:

Having one or more motor tics (for example, blinking and shrugging) or vocal tics (for example, hum, clear your throat or shout a word or phrase), but not both.

Have tics that occur many times a day almost every day or occasionally for more than a year.

Have tics that have started before age 18.

Having symptoms that are not due to the use of medications or other drugs or due to a condition that may cause tics (for example, seizures, Huntington's disease, or post-viral encephalitis).

Not having received a diagnosis of TS.

Transient Tic Disorder

For a person to receive a diagnosis of transient tic disorder, you must meet the following criteria:

Have one or more motor tics (e.g., blink and shrug) or vocal tics (e.g., hum, clear the throat or shout a word or a phrase).

Having had tics for no more than 12 months in a row.

Have tics that have started before age 18.

Have symptoms that are not due to the use of medications or other drugs or a condition that may cause tics (e.g., Huntington's disease or post viral encephalitis).

Not having received a diagnosis of TS or persistent motor or a vocal tic disorder.

Substance/ Medication-Induced Psychotic Disorder

Hallucinations and/or delusions characterize psychotic disorder induced by substances/medications due to the direct effects of a substance or the withdrawal of a substance in the absence of delirium.

Episodes of substance-induced psychosis are common in emergency departments and crisis centers. There are many triggers, such as alcohol, amphetamines, cannabis, cocaine, hallucinogens, opioids, phencyclidine (PCP), and some sedatives/hypnotics. For it to be considered substance-induced psychosis, hallucinations and delusions must be superior to those that normally accompany simple intoxication or substance withdrawal, although the patient may also be intoxicated or suffering from abstinence.

The symptoms are usually brief, they disappear shortly after the effect of the drug ends, but the psychosis caused by amphetamines, cocaine, or PCP can persist for several weeks. Because some young people with schizophrenia in the prodromal or initial phase consume substances that can induce psychosis, it is important to obtain all background information, particularly to explore evidence of previous mental symptoms, before concluding that acute psychosis is due to substance abuse.

Treatment

In most psychoses induced by substances, discontinuing the substance and administering an anxiolytic or antipsychotic drug is effective.

For psychosis due to dopamine stimulant drugs, such as amphetamine, an antipsychotic drug is most effective.

For psychosis due to drugs like LSD, mere observation may be all that needs to be done.

For substances with actions that do not involve dopamine, observation may be all that is needed, or an anxiolytic may be useful.

The main characteristic of this disorder is the presence of hallucinations or delusions that are considered direct effects of a substance, be it a drug, a medication, or a toxic. Hallucinations should not be included when the subject is aware that they are caused by the said substance. The alteration is not better explained by the presence of a psychotic disorder not induced by substances. The diagnosis is not established without the psychotic symptoms only appear in the course of a delirium.

The diagnosis of substance-induced psychotic disorder should only be made if the symptoms are excessive in relation to those usually associated with the withdrawal syndrome, and when the symptoms are of sufficient severity to merit clinical attention.

This disorder only occurs in association with states of intoxication or withdrawal but may persist for weeks, while in primary psychotic disorders may precede the onset of substance use or may occur after long periods of abstinence. Once initiated, the symptoms can continue while the consumption of the substance lasts.

It has been suggested that 9 out of 10 non-auditory hallucinations are the product of a psychotic disorder induced by substances or a psychotic disorder due to medical illness. Care must also be taken, because even in a person with intoxication or abstinence other possible causes of psychotic symptoms have to be taken into account, since, among other things, problems due to substance use are not uncommon among people with disorders psychotic (not induced by substances).

Specific Substances

The substances that can trigger psychotic disorders are: alcohol, hallucinogens, amphetamines, and substances of similar action; cannabis, cocaine, phencyclidine, and substances with similar action; inhalants; opioids (meperidine); sedatives, hypnotics and anxiolytics, and other substances or unknown.

Psychotic symptoms may also occur due to abstinence from these substances: alcohol; sedatives, hypnotics and anxiolytics; and other substances and unknown.

The onset of these symptoms varies depending on the substance. The hallucinations that occur can be in any form. However, the most common in the absence of delirium is auditory. Amphetamine and cocaine poisoning share clinical characteristics. The psychotic disorder induced by cannabis can appear by the consumption of large quantities and are usually delusional thoughts of persecution, but apparently, it is a rare disorder. There may also be marked anxiety, emotional ability, depersonalization, and amnesia after the episode. All this usually remits in 1 day, but sometimes, it lasts a few more days.

It may happen that substance-induced psychotic disorders do not resolve quickly after removing the agent that causes them. When this happens, it is difficult to differentiate this picture from psychotic disorders is induced by substances.

Some medications can cause psychotic symptoms, including anesthetics, analgesics, anticholinergic agents, anticonvulsants, antihistamines, anti-hypertensives, cardiovascular medications, antimicrobials, anti-Parkinson agents, chemotherapeutic agents, corticosteroids, gastrointestinal medications, muscle relaxants, non-steroidal anti-inflammatory drugs, free dispensation, antidepressants and disulfiram.

Differential Diagnosis

A diagnosis of substance-induced psychotic disorder should only be made in lieu of a diagnosis of substance intoxication or substance withdrawal when psychotic symptoms are excessive in relation to those commonly associated with the intoxication or withdrawal syndromes and when the symptoms are of sufficient severity to merit independent clinical attention.

If the judgment of reality remains intact, this disorder cannot be diagnosed. In its place should appear the diagnosis of intoxication due to or withdrawal of substances, with perceptual alterations. Hallucinatory flashbacks that may seem long after using hallucinogens are diagnosed as a persistent perceptual disorder by hallucinogens.

If the psychotic symptoms appear exclusively during delirium, these psychotic symptoms are considered a symptom associated with delirium. The psychotic disorder induced by substances of the primary psychotic disorder must be differentiated very well since it is this second disorder that is not a substance that causes the symptoms.

A psychotic disorder induced by substances due to a treatment prescribed for a medical or mental illness should be initiated while the subject is taking the medication. When the treatment has been interrupted, the psychotic symptoms should subside after a few days or a few weeks, depending on the half-life of the substance consumed; But if the symptoms persist beyond four weeks, other possible causes should be considered. Sometimes a change of medication is necessary to see if the medication is the causative agent. If the clinician verifies that the alteration is due both to medical illness and to the consumption of some substance, then both diagnoses must be given.

When the data are not sufficient to determine if certain substances produce the symptoms, or if they are primary symptoms, or if they are due to a medical disease, an unspecified psychotic disorder will be determined.

Relationship with the Research Diagnostic Criteria of the ICD-10

ICD-10 divides this disorder into two categories: 1) psychotic disorder due to the use of psychoactive substances if symptoms appear during the first two weeks of consumption; and 2) psychotic disorder of late-onset to the consumption of psychoactive substances if the symptoms appear between 2 and six weeks after starting the consumption. In this classification, a minimum duration of 6 months is required.

Catatonia

It is possible that we have ever seen in a movie, read in a book or even seen in real life some psychiatric patients who remain in a state of absence, rigid and immobile, mute and unreactive, and can be placed by third parties in any imaginable position and remaining in that position as a wax doll.

This condition is what is known as catatonia, a mainly motor syndrome of diverse causes that affects patients with different types of mental and medical disorders.

Catatonia as a syndrome: concept and symptoms

Catatonia is a neuropsychological syndrome in which a series of psychomotor symptoms occur, often accompanied by cognitive alterations, of conscience and perception.

Your diagnosis requires at least three of the symptoms above, for at least twenty-four hours. As a general rule, anosognosia is presented concerning motor symptomatology.

Some Psychological Symptoms

The subjects with this alteration often present an intense emotionality, difficult to control, both positively and negatively. Although motor immobility is characteristic, patients sometimes leave it in an emotional state of great intensity and with a high level of movement and agitation that can lead them to self-harm or to attack others. Despite their anosognosia regarding their motor symptoms, they are nonetheless aware of their emotions and the intensity with which they present themselves.

Catatonia can occur in different degrees of greater or lesser severity, producing alterations in the patient's vital functioning that can make it difficult to adapt to the environment.

Although the prognosis is good if it starts to be treated soon, in some cases, it can be chronic and can even be fatal in certain circumstances.

Patterns of presentation

Two typical patterns of the presentation can be observed, one called stuporous or slowed catatonia and another known as agitated or delirious catatonia.

The first of them is characterized by a state of stupor in which there is an absence of functions related to the environment; the individual remains paralyzed and absent from the environment, the common symptoms being catalepsy, waxy flexibility, mutism, and negativism.

Concerning agitated or delirious catatonia, it is characterized by symptoms more linked to activation such as eco symptoms, the performance of stereotyped movements, and states of agitation.

Possible causes of catatonia

The causes of catatonia can be very diverse. When considering neuropsychological syndrome, the presence of alterations in the nervous system must be taken into account.

Research shows that patients with catatonia have some dysfunction in part of the right posterior parietal cortex, which is consistent with the fact that people with catatonia can initiate movements correctly (so that the supplementary motor area usually remains preserved), and the fact that there is anosognosia concerning motor symptoms. The inferior lateral prefrontal of these subjects also usually presents alterations, as well as the medial orbitofrontal, which also explains the presence of occasional raptus and emotional alterations.

A hormonal level explores the role of GABA, which has been revealed altered in patients with catatonia to present a lower level of attachment to brain structures. Glutamate, serotonin, and dopamine also seem to play a relevant role in this disorder, but a greater level of research is needed as to exactly how they influence.

Potential Organic Causes

One of the first causes that should be explored first is the organic type since catatonia is a symptom present in a large number of neurological disorders. In this sense, we can find that epilepsy of the temporal lobe, encephalitis, brain tumors, and cerebrovascular accidents are possible causes of this syndrome that should be treated immediately.

In addition to infections such as septicemia or those caused by tuberculosis, malaria, syphilis, or HIV can also cause this state. Liver and kidney failure, hypothyroidism, severe complications of diabetes such as ketoacidosis, or even severe hypothermia, are other conditions that have been linked to the onset of catatonia.

Other biological causes can be derived from the consumption and/or abuse of psychoactive substances, whether drugs or psychotropic drugs. For example, catatonia frequently appears in neuroleptic malignant syndrome, a serious and potentially fatal syndrome that, in some cases, appears when antipsychotics are administered.

Causes from psychodynamics

In addition to the above causes, some authors related to the Freudian tradition have proposed that in some cases catatonia may have psychological aspects of a symbolic nature as a cause.

Specifically, it has been proposed that catatonia may appear as a regression to a primitive state as a defense mechanism against traumatic or frightening stimuli. The explanation that it can also occur as a dissociation response (which is observed in some patients with post-traumatic stress disorder) is also used.

However, it must be borne in mind that these explanations are based on an epistemology far removed from the scientific, and therefore are no longer considered valid.

Mental Disorders in Which It Appears

Catatonia has long been a syndrome that has been identified with a subtype of schizophrenia, catatonic schizophrenia. However, the presence of this syndrome has also been observed in numerous disorders, both mental and organic.

Some of the different disorders to which it has appeared linked are the following.

1. Schizophrenia and other psychotic disorders

This is the type of condition to which catatonia has traditionally been linked, to the point that catatonia has been considered as a specific subtype of schizophrenia. Apart from schizophrenia can appear in other disorders such as brief psychotic disorder.

2. Mood disorders

Although it has been linked almost since its inception with schizophrenia, the different studies carried out concerning catatonia seem to indicate that a high number of Catatonic patients present some mood disorders, especially in manic or depressive episodes. It can be specified in both depressive and bipolar disorders.

3. Posttraumatic Stress Disorder

Posttraumatic Stress Disorder has also occasionally been associated with catatonic states.

4. Consumption, intoxication or withdrawal of substances

The administration or uncontrolled cessation of certain substances with an effect on the encephalon can generate catatonia.

5. Autistic spectrum disorder

Some children with developmental disorders such as autism may manifest catatonia comorbidly.

Consideration Today

Today the latest revision of one of the main psychology diagnostic manuals, the DSM-5, has eliminated this label as a subtype of schizophrenia to convert the catatonia in an indicator or modifier of the diagnosis of this and other disorders (such as mood). The classification as a neuropsychological syndrome has been added separately from other disorders.

Treatment to be applied

Because the etiology (causes) of catatonia can be diverse, the treatments to be applied will depend to a great extent on what produces it. Its origin must be analyzed and act differently according to what it is. Apart from this, the symptoms of catatonia can be treated in different ways.

At a pharmacological level, the high utility of benzodiazepines, which act as agonists of GABA in acute cases, has been proven. The effects of this treatment can end up reversing the symptoms of most patients. One of the most effective shown is lorazepam, which is, in fact, the treatment of the first choice.

While it may seem due to its link with schizophrenia that the application of antipsychotics may be useful, the truth is that it can be harmful (remember that catatonia can appear in the neuroleptic malignant syndrome that is precisely caused by the administration of said drugs).

Another therapy used is electroconvulsive therapy, although it is usually applied if treatment with benzodiazepines does not provoke a response. It also raises the possibility of using together benzodiazepines and electroconvulsive therapy, to be able to enhance the effects.

At the psychological level, occupational therapy can be performed to stimulate the patient, as well as psychoeducation for the patient and their environment in order to provide them with information and strategies for action and prevention. The treatment of affective symptoms is also very helpful, especially in cases derived from psychiatric disorders.

Today, society has made significant progress in understanding mental illness. In the beginning, it was considered that a person with a mental illness, could be someone "touched" by the gods, which gives them a power of understanding of an ethereal world that escapes our rational understanding; going through the conception that instead of gods, that capacity of the "enlightened" would be more referred to demons and pacts with the devil; the use of mechanisms for their control such as deprivation of freedom, electroshocks, among others, and reaching our days, in which it is common for us to refer lightly to a partner and tell him that sounds paranoid to say that there could be a global conspiracy of governments to control society, catalog of schizophrenics to those who claim to have had a vision of a deceased family member or with attention deficit disorder, whom one perceives as hyperactive and with little ability to concentrate in the performance of their work at a given moment (It should be noted that even many of these primitive beliefs about mental illness and treatment methods are maintained today and are determined according to the level of evolution of each culture).

This case also happens with bipolarity. The term has become popular to the point that as a society, we say that a person, say a boss who a few minutes ago shared a funny anecdote with his subordinates and after a while is in a bad mood and irritable, giving orders and demanding concentration at work Without an apparent reason, he suffers from bipolar disorder. However, not always this understanding that we have about mental illnesses is enough to identify them in ourselves or in a third party. While it is true that bipolarity involves a disorder in which there are alterations in mood, this involves a set of criteria that at a clinical level must be present to assert, this time with firmness and without lightness that a person suffers from this disease mental.

Bipolar Disorder

Bipolar disorder, formerly called Manic-Depressive Psychosis, is a mental illness characterized by the cyclical and recurrent presence of a set of disorders, which present intense phases of alterations in mood.

Due to the complexity, intensity and variety of emotional states that the human experiences every day, the Diagnostic and Statistical Manual of Mental Disorders, better known as DSM-V, classifies Bipolar Disorder in two different manifestations:

Bipolar II disorder - It is a mental disorder characterized by the presence of a Manic Episode.

Bipolar II Disorder - It is a mental disorder characterized by the presence of one or several Hypomanic Episodes and one or several Episodes of Major Depression that precede or continue to the Hypomanic Episodes.

This definition indicates that, in effect, it is necessary that both episodes have been present in the subject's life: Hypomanic Episode and Episode of Major Depression. While in Bipolar I Disorder, it is only necessary that the Manic Episode be presented for identification.

From these definitions of the types of Bipolar Disorders, we extract three terms that are vital to distinguish the presence of an intense alteration in the mood of a person, and that will allow us to distinguish between a Bipolar I Disorder and Bipolar II Disorder. These are: Manic Episode, Hypomanic Episode, and Episode of Major Depression. Let us know the clinical diagnostic criteria that the DSM-V indicates for each one of these episodes of alteration in the state of mind.

Diagnostic Criteria of the Manic Episode

A. - Presence during the minimum period of one week and during most of the day, almost every day, of an abnormal and persistently elevated, expansive or irritable mood, as well as activity or energy. In the case of requiring hospitalization, any period of duration of this elevated state of mind and activity will be considered.

B.- The presence of three or more of the following symptoms to a significant degree that represents a marked change in their daily behavior (four if the mood is only irritable), that have been present during the period of high activity and state of an abnormally high mood:

1. Feelings of Greatness or increase of self-esteem.

2. Decrease in the need to sleep (3 hours of sleep are enough).

3. Pressure to keep the conversation or more talkative than usual.

4. Leakage of ideas or subjective experience that your thoughts are going fast.

5. It is easily distracted by irrelevant external stimuli.

6. Increase of the activity directed to an objective (social, labor, school or sexual) or psychomotor agitation (Activity not directed to a purpose).

7. Excessive participation in activities whose possibilities of painful consequences is high (unrestrained shopping activities, chance, sexual indiscretions, or imprudent investments of money).

C.- This alteration of the mood causes a significant deterioration in the social or work functioning of the individual, requires hospitalization to prevent the subject from harming himself or others, or presents psychotic characteristics.

D.- This important alteration of mood cannot be attributed to the physiological effects of any substance (drugs, medications, treatments) or to another medical condition.

Diagnostic Criteria of the Hypomanic Episode

A.- Presence during the minimum period of four consecutive days and during most of the day, almost every day, of an abnormal and persistently elevated, expansive or irritable mood, as well as activity or energy. In the case of requiring hospitalization, any period of duration of this elevated state of mind and activity will be considered.

B.- The presence of three or more of the following symptoms to a significant degree that represents a marked change in their daily behavior (four if the mood is only irritable), that have been present during the period of high activity and state of an abnormally high mood:

1. Feelings of Greatness or increase of self-esteem.

2. Decrease in the need to sleep (3 hours of sleep are enough).

3. Pressure to keep the conversation or more talkative than usual.

4. Leakage of ideas or subjective experience that your thoughts are going fast.

5. It is easily distracted by irrelevant external stimuli.

6. Increase of the activity directed to an objective (social, labor, school or sexual) or psychomotor agitation (Activity not directed to a purpose).

7. Excessive participation in activities whose possibilities of painful consequences is high (unrestrained shopping

activities, chance, sexual indiscretions, or imprudent investments of money).

C.- The change in the functioning associated with this episode is not characteristic when the individual does not present symptoms.

D.- The alteration of mood and change in functioning are observable by other people.

E.- The episode does not cause significant alteration of the social or work functioning of the subject or requires hospitalization.

F. - This important alteration of the state of mind cannot be attributed to the physiological effects of any substance (drugs, medications, treatments).

Diagnostic Criteria for Major Depression Episode

A.- During the two-week period, at least five (or more) of the following symptoms must be present, in which at least one symptom of depressed mood or loss of interest or pleasure is present.

Note: These symptoms cannot be due to another medical condition.

1. Depressed mood almost every day for most of the day, according to subjective information (feeling empty, sad or hopeless) or observation by third parties (The tearful person is seen). In children and adolescents, the state of mind may be irritable.

2. Decreased pleasure or interest in almost all activities during most of the day, almost every day.

3. Increase or significant loss of weight that is not due to a diet or diet in particular (more than 5% of body mass in a month) or increases or decreases in appetite almost every day. In children, it is observed with a failure to achieve the expected weight gain.

4. Insomnia or hypersomnia almost every day.

5. Agitation or psychomotor retardation almost every day (It is required to be observable by third parties and not only by the subjective feeling of the person).

6. Fatigue or loss of energy almost every day.

7. Feelings of feeling useless or of excessive or inappropriate guilt (which can be delusional) almost every day (Excluding self-reproach or guilt for feeling sick).

8. Reduces the ability to make decisions, to think or to concentrate almost every day.

9. Recurrent thoughts of death, recurring ideas, and suicide without a determined plan, a suicide attempt, or a specific plan to carry it out.

B.- These symptoms cause a significant and significant deterioration in the social functioning, work, or other areas of the individual.

C.- This episode cannot be attributed to the physiological effects of any substance or other medical condition.

In the case of the Major Depression Episode, it is essential that the psychologist or psychiatrist consider whether this reaction could have been due to a significant loss to the subject (Death of a family member, divorce, considerable economic loss, serious disability or illness) and qualify if the symptoms that the person experiences are the adequate ones for said situation or on the contrary, the presentation of these symptoms are not associated to any of these events and even, if they are proper expressions of the culture of the subject. Clinical criteria will be vital in these cases.

The clinical description of Bipolar Disorder

People diagnosed with Bipolar Disorder in a Manic Episode can quickly change from one emotional state to another, such as from joy to rage, without the same subject noticing the situation. The discourse of these people is branched, grandiose, and can present a flight of ideas and delusions that could lead to the suicide attempt.

A pattern of risky behaviors can be observed, such as the presence of overt hypersexuality, in which inadequate sexual desires and fantasies and very naked clothing stand out in order to sexually provoke other people; increase in the consumption of psychotropic substances and the abandonment of the treatment due to not being considered ill.

The manic state can be dangerous because the subject could get to attack those who are close to him or himself. From there to that in case of manifesting this type of behavior, quickly inform your trusted psychologist so that the person is treated urgently and / or hospitalized to stabilize their symptoms.

In the case of people diagnosed with Bipolar Disorder in Hypomanic Episode, the language is characterized by being verbose. However, it does not lead to the flight of ideas, the desire to obtain pleasure remains, there are no delusions, and there is no deterioration of social and labor activity as in mania.

These episodes begin suddenly, in moments one becomes aware of the use of a high tone of voice or the excess of makeup in the case of women.

From the psychoanalytic point of view, it is considered that the manic and hypomanic episodes are defenses of the self that the person uses in an unconscious way before his unconscious feeling of disability, denying the dependency relationship with the object, anxiety, guilt and an internal duel that the subject has not processed. This defense mechanism arises possibly due to an excessive erogenization fixed in the oral psychosexual stage of the subject. This duel is not necessarily linked to a real or physical duel for the loss of a loved one. This could also refer to mourning for feeling abandoned by their parents (Even when they are alive and living with them) or another unconscious internal mourning. Hence, in general, the manifestation of a manic or hypomanic episode in the subject's life usually precedes or continues to episodes of major depression. The manic defenses act as a protector of the ego in the unconscious feeling of disability that the depressive episodes show. From here, to that in a certain way, they are the two poles of the same disorder.

Causes and Risk Factors of Bipolar Disorder

Hereditary factors: There is evidence of a strong genetic influence as a cause and a risk factor for Bipolar Disorder. The risk of an adult having Bipolar Disorder is 10 times higher if they have a relative with a diagnosis of Bipolar Disorder. The magnitude of the risk increases if it is a direct family member.

Neurological factors: At the moment, there is no certainty of which neurotransmitters are likely to affect the biochemistry of the brain and are associated with these important fluctuations in the mood of the person. Although it is a broad field of study, current research in this regard can help us unveil it promptly.

Environmental factors: If the person has a certain genetic or biochemical disposition regarding bipolar disorder and experiences that may be traumatic or lead a life whose level of anxiety and stress is high; it will provide the necessary catalyst for this disorder to detonate.

Differential Factors of Bipolar Disorder

Cyclothymia: This disorder is a chronic and fluctuating alteration of the state of mind that entails numerous periods of hypomanic symptoms and periods of depressive symptoms, different from each other. However, they are insufficient in number, severity, generalization, or duration to meet the criteria of Bipolar Disorder I or Bipolar II Disorder. For diagnosis, these episodes of mood disturbance should manifest during the first two years (one year in the case of children and adolescents), and there should not be a period between episodes greater than two months.

Major Depressive Disorder: There is a high overlap between the symptoms of both disorders because as we saw that the person affected with Bipolar I disorder could have had or could have a Major Depressive Episode, it is also possible that a person with Major Depressive Episode manifests symptoms similar to mania or hypomania. However, the difference of the latter lies in the fact that the manic and hypomanic symptoms presented in the Major Depression Disorder do not meet all the diagnostic criteria, such as the number of symptoms or the duration of these.

Personality Limit Disorder: They have an important overlap between the symptoms, due to effective ability and frequent impulsivity in both disorders, however, in the case of Bipolar Disorder, the symptoms must suppose a different episode and the appreciable increase in the behaviors of the subject must be observed, which will differ from your normal mood. Remember that all Personality Disorder is characterized by the stability of a set of patterns of behavior that differs significantly from what is accepted as normal in society.

Schizophrenia and Spectrum Disorders of Schizophrenia: The overlapping of symptoms among these disorders is that, although there may be manifestations of psychotic symptoms and delusions in Bipolar Disorder, in the case of Schizophrenia and spectrum disorders of schizophrenia, these symptoms appear in the absence of symptoms affective prominent.

Attention Deficit / Hyperactivity Disorder (ADHD): This confusion arises mainly because there is an overlap of ADHD in children and adolescents with Bipolar II Disorder in symptoms such as: Verborrhea, acceleration of thought, high distraction and less need for sleep. However, as with the Personality Disorder, the psychologist must clarify whether the symptoms represent a considerable elevation of mood and are characteristic of a specific episode or, on the contrary, part of a stable pattern of behaviors. It is important to note that numerous scientific studies indicate that there may be a correlation between ADHD in children and the emergence of Bipolar Disorder once they are adults. Because this study deserves a longitudinal investigation (Since the child is diagnosed with ADHD until an adult is diagnosed with Bipolar Disorder), it will take some years for us to have several reliable investigations that allow us to affirm or contradict with accuracy this correlation.

Treatments for Bipolar Disorder

Due to the intensity of emotions experienced by these patients during their manic, hypomanic and / or depressive episodes, it is essential to attend when they include psychotic states that highlight delusions and acting out or low impulse controls, which could prompt them to illegal actions, of aggression towards other people or towards themselves (suicides and / or self-harm). If these behaviors are present, hospitalization and the use of drugs will be a priority.

Pharmacological: It is the main treatment to consider in case of presenting this disorder and is of vital importance due to the importance of counteracting the symptoms in manic episodes in which the subject could attempt against his life or against others, either by a manifestation of delusional ideas or suicidal ideation. In depressive episodes, the risk of suicide is something due to the high internal devaluation that it has of itself. These treatments usually consist of the combination of mood-stabilizing drugs, antipsychotics, and antidepressants, depending on the episode of mood alteration that the subject presents.

Behavioral Cognitive Therapy: Among the purposes of this therapy is to adhere patients to pharmacological medication, as well as the acquisition of skills that allow them to reduce the problems generated by Bipolar Disorder.

Psychoanalysis or Psychodynamic Therapy: This therapeutic approach is of vital importance for the person affected with Bipolar Disorder since as mentioned in this article, mania is an unconscious defense mechanism that the Ego uses to protect itself from depression. Psychoanalysis will allow the subject to acquire the unconscious understanding that covers his episodes of alteration of moods and to deepen in those internal experiences that will allow him, now consciously, to integrate and strengthen his Self and self-regulate its fluctuations or the possible occurrence of these episodes. Because it is preferable for the patient to manifest Insight's ability to apply this therapy, it is more appropriate if it is applied once the symptoms of the manic, hypomanic or major depressive episode have subsided.

Psychoeducation: It implies psychoeducational and emotional work in conjunction with parents and immediate family members in order to confront this situation in a joint manner. It is important to note that the emergence of mental illness involves a strong change for both the affected person and their family and friends. Therefore, these psychoeducational programs should be oriented to provide emotional and coping tools for bipolar disorder for both, in addition to being support for adherence to the treatment of individuals with this diagnosis.

Support Network: This network includes direct relatives and friendships of the person, contacts of the psychotherapist and emergency care centers, etc. As well as people who can take care of children in case the patient has them and is in crisis. This will allow address the manifestation of an episode of mood alteration and have important links that allow quick and effective control.

Bipolar disorder is undoubtedly one of the mental illnesses with the greatest impact on the family and social level. Considering the high emotional cost that this exerts on the person and their family, risks that could arise if this disease is not detected or treated in time.

Promiscuous behaviors, suicide risks, antisocial behaviors, long recovery time and disqualification functional of the individual in society are all notable side effects.

Cyclothymic Disorder

Cyclothymic disorder is an alteration of the chronic mood and with variations that include alternate periods of hypomania and mild depression.

In this disorder, both hypomanic and depressive symptoms are not numerous enough, nor serious, nor are they sufficiently important or long enough to be considered as a manic or major depressive episode.

We define the hypomanic episode as an abnormal state of mind and continually exalted, euphoric, or irritable for a period of time of at least 4 days. In this period, in addition to this characteristic, there must be at least three other symptoms such as an increase in self-esteem, a verbose language, psychomotor agitation, lack of concentration, insomnia, etc. The hypomanic episode differs from the maniac in the absence of delusional ideas and hallucinations and that, in both, important changes occur in the habitual activity of those who suffer it.

However, in the hypomanic, the changes are not so serious as to cause significant social and occupational deterioration or to require hospitalization.

We define the depressive episode as the one whose main characteristic is a mood or depressive mood, together with a diminished interest in things and gives the ability to enjoy, insomnia or hypersomnia, fatigue or loss of energy almost all day, feeling guilt or uselessness, loss of appetite, etc.

We define mixed episodes as the coexistence of episodes of hypomanic and depressive symptoms at the same time.

Duration and diagnosis

It has a period of approximately two years, in which the symptoms last less than two months in total.

It is only considered cyclothymic disorder if, in this period of time, there is no manic episode, major depression or mixed.

It is not considered cyclothymic disorder when the symptoms it presents and the alteration of mood are due to the effects produced by a drug, medication, any treatment for depression or by any toxic substance, or when the symptoms are due to a medical disease.

If after two years there are manic or mixed episodes superimposed on the cyclothymic disorder, then both the cyclothymic disorder and the bipolar disorder will be diagnosed.

Similarly, if major depressive episodes superimposed on the cyclothymic disorder occur, both disorders will be diagnosed.

Course

This disorder usually begins at an early age, in adolescence or at the beginning of adulthood.

It occurs more frequently in women than in men, approximately in a proportion of three women for every two men and, in general, women tend to submit more easily than men to medical treatment.

Normally, they have a deceptive and confusing start, as well as a chronic and irregular course.

There is a 15-50% risk that people with cyclothymic disorder will develop a bipolar disorder.

Symptoms

Changes in mood occur abruptly and irregularly, and with many periods of euphoria and depression, there may be periods in which the symptoms do not appear, although not necessarily.

Those who suffer from it often feel that they cannot control their mood, which irritates them even more.

The periods of depression and euphoria do not meet criteria regarding the duration and intensity of manic episodes, major or mixed depressive.

In the hypomanic episodes, in addition to the euphoric and exalted state that characterizes it, there must be at least three symptoms of the following:

- Presence of greater energy and increased activity and vitality.
- Alterations of sleep with a decrease in the need to sleep.
- Increase in social relations, a greater predisposition to carry out activities, and an increase in interest in things.
- Appearance of a verbose language.
- Greater psychomotor agitation.
- Increase in self-esteem
- Exaggerated optimism.

Likewise, in depressive episodes one must present, in addition to mood or depressive mood, three of the following symptoms:

- Absence of energy and decrease in activity and vitality.
- Insomnia.
- Cessation of social relations and social isolation, along with great lack of interest in things and activities.
- Decreased appetite.
- Decrease in self-esteem and negative attitudes and thoughts about your life and everything about yourself and

those around you.

Depressive Disorders

Depressive disorders are characterized by the sadness of intensity or duration sufficient to interfere with the functionality and, sometimes, a decrease in interest or pleasure aroused by the activities. The exact cause is unknown but probably has to do with inheritance, changes in neurotransmitter concentrations, an alteration in neuroendocrine function, and psychosocial factors. The diagnosis is based on the anamnesis. In the treatment, drugs or psychotherapy are used and, sometimes, electroconvulsive therapy.

The term depression is used specially to refer to any of the depressive disorders. In the fifth edition of the Diagnostic and Statistical Manual of Mental Disorders (DSM-5), some types of disorders are classified according to the specific symptoms:

Depressive disorders can occur at any age, but their development is typical. adolescence and between 20 and 30 years. Up to 30% of patients report depressive symptoms in primary care centers, but 10% will have major depression.

Demoralization And Punishment

The term depression is often used to describe a low or discouraged state of mind resulting from disappointments (e.g., financial crises, natural disasters, serious illness) or loss (e.g., death). of a loved one). However, the most appropriate terms for these moods are demoralization and grief.

The negative feelings of demoralization and sadness, unlike depression, occur in waves that are usually linked to thoughts or memories of the triggering event, are resolved when circumstances or events improve, can be interspersed with periods of positive emotion and humor, and are not accompanied by penetrating feelings of worthlessness and self-hatred. Depressed mood usually lasts days instead of weeks or months, and suicidal thoughts and prolonged loss of functionality are much less likely.

However, the events and stressors that induce demoralization and grief may also precipitate a major depressive episode, particularly in vulnerable people (e.g., those with a family history or background of major depression).

Etiology

The exact cause of depressive disorders is unknown, but genetic and environmental factors contribute.

Inheritance accounts for 50% of the etiology (less in the so-called late-onset depression). Therefore, depression is more frequent among first-degree relatives of patients with this condition; the agreement between identical twins is high. In addition, genetic factors probably influence the development of depressive responses to adverse events.

Psychosocial factors may also be involved. Situations of major stress in daily life, especially separations and losses, usually precede episodes of major depression; however, these events do not usually cause intense depression of long duration, except in people predisposed to suffer a mood disorder.

People who have had an episode of major depression have a higher risk of suffering other episodes in the future. People less flexible and / or with anxiety tendencies are more likely to develop a depressive disorder because they lack the social skills necessary to adjust to the pressures of life. Depression can also appear in people who have other mental illnesses.

Women have a higher risk, but there is no theory that explains why. Possible factors include the following:

Increased exposure or greater response to daily stress

Higher levels of monoamine oxidase (the enzyme that degrades neurotransmitters is considered important for mood)

Higher rates of thyroid dysfunction

Endocrine changes produce with menstruation and menopause

In postpartum depression, symptoms appear during pregnancy or within 4 weeks after delivery (postpartum depression); the participation of endocrine factors is involved, but the specific cause is unknown.

In seasonal affective disorder, symptoms develop following a seasonal pattern, typically in autumn or winter; the disorder tends to appear in climates that have long or raw winters.

Depressive symptoms or disorders can appear in several physical disorders, including thyroid and adrenal disorders, benign and malignant brain tumors, stroke, AIDS, Parkinson's disease, and multiple sclerosis.

Some drugs, such as corticosteroids, some beta-blockers, interferon, reserpine, can also cause depressive disorders. The abuse of some substances for recreational use (e.g., alcohol, amphetamines) can cause or accompany depression. Toxic effects or abstinence can cause transient depressive symptoms.

Sometimes, we feel a certain level of anxiety or worry when facing certain types of challenges in our life. From babies, this anxiety we experience when we separate from our mother and from there, to each new and unknown situation that has been presented to us (First day of classes, evaluations, medical exams, new employment, etc.). These new opportunities and challenges have allowed us to be more and more capable of solving problems and allows us not only to face them successfully but also to face new challenges with a higher level of demand and complexity, while at the same time boosting our integral development.

However, there are moments in our lives in which this high level of anxiety manifests itself constantly, affecting us physically, we get tired with great ease, we get irritated by everyday aspects of everyday life and enter a circle from which we cannot find a way out , even to develop a constant state of alert and to feel that we do not have the tools to face the new situations in our lives. When these conditions occur, it is very likely that we are developing some type of anxiety disorder, that if not addressed promptly, we could develop other types of pathologies such as phobias, somatizations, etc.

Anxiety is a mental state that allows our mind and body to prepare for flight or combat when facing a different situation and from which we could consider some level of danger. From the clinical point of view, we can define Anxiety, as a state of mind in which the subject, faced with the possibility of facing some danger or misfortune in the future, feels a markedly negative, apprehensive affect and with bodily manifestations of tension.

Anxiety Disorders

Due to the diversity of circumstantial factors in the face of anxiety or fear, the Diagnostic and Statistical Manual of Mental Disorders, also known as DSM-5, establishes a classification of anxiety disorders, which will allow us to facilitate both their identification, as the appropriate treatment.

Separation Anxiety Disorder: It is an anxiety disorder characterized by the manifestation of fear and excessive and inappropriate anxiety in relation to their separation from those people towards whom they feel attachment.

Selective Mutism: an Anxiety disorder characterized by the constant manifestation of difficulties when speaking in specific social situations, despite being able to do it in other situations in an adequate manner.

Specific Phobia: an Anxiety disorder characterized by the presence of fear or intense anxiety before an object or specific situation: fear of flying, heights, see blood, etc.

Social Anxiety Disorder (Social Phobia): an Anxiety disorder characterized by the presence of fear or intense anxiety in one or more social situations in which the individual is exposed to possible examination by other people: having a conversation, being observed while eating or drinking, giving a talk in front of several people, etc.

Panic disorder: Anxiety disorder characterized by the unforeseen and recurrent manifestation of fear or intense discomfort, which reaches its maximum expression in minutes and characterized, among other criteria, by four or more of the following symptoms: Accelerated palpitation of the heart, sweating, tremor, difficulties for breathing, feeling choked, nausea, feeling dizzy, chills or feeling of heat, tingling or numbness, derealization or depersonalization, fear of "going crazy", fear of dying.

Agoraphobia: an Anxiety disorder characterized by intense anxiety that arises in places or situations where it would be difficult to escape.

Substance / medication-induced Anxiety Disorder: Mental disorder characterized by the presence of panic attacks or excessive anxiety that has been induced by intoxication or withdrawal of substances or medications

Anxiety Disorder due to another medical condition: Mental disorder characterized by the presence of panic attacks or excessive anxiety as a direct pathophysiological consequence of another medical condition.

Another Anxiety Disorder not specified: Mental disorder characterized by the presence of the characteristic signs of an anxiety disorder that causes clinically significant discomfort in important areas of functioning (social, academic, work) but do not meet the criteria of other anxiety disorders.

Generalized Anxiety Disorder: Mental disorder characterized by anxiety and excessive worry in relation to the possible occurrence or anticipation of a series of events or activities (work or school).

Diagnostic Criteria of Generalized Anxiety

The Diagnostic and Statistical Manual of Mental Disorders or DSM-5 defines it as an anxiety disorder characterized by anxiety and excessive concern about a series of events or activities and determines certain specific criteria to consider that a pattern of behavior must be framed as a Disorder of Generalized Anxiety.

A.- This symptomatology must be manifested for more days than those that have been absent, causing clinically significant discomfort in different areas of functioning (social, work, academic) for a minimum period of six months.

B. - The subject is difficult to control the concern.

C.- This anxiety or worry is related to three or more of the following symptoms (In children, only one item is required):

Nerves of tip or feeling of being trapped.

Get fatigued easily

Difficulty to concentrate or have a blank mind.

Muscle tension.

Sleep problems (Unsatisfactory, difficulty falling asleep, or maintaining sleep).

D.- This alteration cannot be attributed to the physiological effects of a substance, nor is it better explained by another mental disorder.

Clinical Description of Generalized Anxiety

The person diagnosed with Generalized Anxiety Disorder manifests an intensity, frequency, and duration disproportionate to the real impact of the event or situation anticipated, interfering with his attention to immediate tasks and often associated with physical symptoms. This concern consumes a great amount of time and energy, which, added to the different physical symptoms that this generates, contributes to a faster deterioration of the subject, even affecting or interfering in the ability to foster trust in the children. While the non-pathological (normal) anxiety does not affect the psychosocial functioning, the subject can be allowed to attend an event that considers more urgent to the one that generates the anxiety, and this is associated with a lower frequency of physical symptoms (restlessness, nervousness).

In adults, many of these concerns are related to day-to-day activities or daily events, whether in their work context, health, finances, family, etc. While in children, disproportionate anxiety is observed when facing competencies that measure their quality or performance in the sports or academic field.

From the physical point of view, people affected with Generalized Anxiety Disorder, can relate the disease with muscular tension, tremors, nervous contractions, instability, and muscular discomfort or pain. Sometimes, these people may also manifest somatic symptoms such as sweating, headaches, nausea, diarrhea, and exaggerated startle reactions. At a lower level of frequency and intensity are the symptoms of vegetative hyperactivity: accelerated heart rate, difficulty breathing, dizziness.

Psychodynamic Understanding of Anxiety

Sigmund Freud, the father of Psychoanalysis, considers that the function of Anxiety is to alert the ego to an instinctive danger so that it activates the defense mechanisms, as well as to drain the surplus of psychic arousal produced by such stimulation so that it can be reduced to a level that allows the homeostatic balance.

At first, anxiety arises from our childhood chronologically: a.- Before the loss of the object, b.- The loss of the love of the object, c.- The fear of castration and d.- Before the fear of censorship and criticism from the superego. These dangers will be consistent throughout our lives, and their intensity will vary according to each individual.

In a sequential manner, we can indicate that the individual, even with apparent good physical health but with important unconscious difficulties, could manifest anxiety before precipitating events such as the increase of external demands and pressures, the mobilization of repressed conflicts and / or a decrease in their capacity to adapt. This generates a weakening of the capacity of the mechanisms of repression to control the unconscious conflicts that are desired do not break into consciousness, thus generating a homeostatic imbalance generated by the symptoms and diagnostic and descriptive criteria already discussed of the Anxiety, in conjunction with Regression of the current triggering problems to early childhood conflicts. Therefore, the subject must unconsciously resort to other Defense Mechanisms such as Rationalization, which allows him to consider the affected subject, that Anxiety is produced by some somatic illness and Displacement, generating that this Anxiety in effect, direct towards an organ or system and manage to reduce the anxiety load but increasing the somatic manifestations. When these anxieties, instead of being displaced towards the body, are directed towards situations, animals or things, what we know as Phobias develop.

Causes and Risk Factors of Generalized Anxiety

Biological Factors: It affects a third of the risk of suffering from this disease, and its genetic factors present an important overlap with the risk of neuroticism, other anxiety disorders, and mood disorders, especially Major Depressive Disorder. A great influence of the neurotransmitter GABA has been identified, which reduces the activity of the central nervous system, so the use of selective serotonin reuptake inhibitors (SSRIs), used for the pharmacological treatment of depression, allow alleviating anxiety by directly acting on this neurotransmitter.

Psychosocial factors: Maintaining a stressful lifestyle for prolonged periods, going through pressing situations from the point of financial or family life, facing a chronic illness or going through a life crisis, together with a certain genetic predisposition, would lead to the symptomatic manifestation of this mental disorder. The abuse of substances such as alcohol, caffeine, cannabis (marijuana), cocaine, and anxiolytics, are closely related to the emergence or increase of anxiety levels.

Differential Factors of Generalized Anxiety

Social Anxiety Disorder. These subjects express their anxiety before social situations close to or when they are evaluated by third parties, while those affected by Generalized Anxiety Disorder can express their concern whether they are being evaluated or not.

Obsessive Compulsive Disorder. In OCD, obsessions are generated by giving intrusive and unwanted thought forms, impulses, or images to inappropriate ideas that arise. While in Generalized Anxiety Disorder, excessive worry focuses on future problems.

Post Traumatic Stress Disorder and Adaptation Disorders. The level of anxiety is invariably present in these three disorders. The differential factor is given as to whether this anxiety meets the criteria of Post Traumatic Stress or Adjustment Disorder. Among some of these differentiating criteria regarding Post Traumatic Stress we have: Actual exposure or threat to death, serious injury or sexual violence; memories and anguished and recurrent dreams associated with traumatic events subsequent to the traumatic event. While in the Adaptation Disorder, anxiety is the response that precedes for three months the appearance of a stressor that has been identified and this anxiety lasts for more than six months after the disappearance of the stressor or its consequences.

Depressive, Bipolar, and Psychotic Disorders. Generalized anxiety and worry should not be diagnosed separately if it only appears during the course of these disorders, as it is a common quality in depressive, bipolar, and psychotic disorders.

Generalized Anxiety Treatments

Brief Dynamic Psychotherapy. Sometimes, the level of anxiety will be so high and intense that it will merit the intervention of the psychologist through a Brief, Intensive and Urgent Psychotherapy that manages to establish the conditions to be able to implement later, a psychotherapy of greater duration, that allows to face and to understand not only the elements that sustain the exogenous anguish or the endogenous anguish with preconscious elements, but to deepen to the unconscious level. As a basis for Brief Dynamic Psychotherapy, the psychoanalyst Leopold Bellak establishes a set of criteria that the therapist should consider in cases of intense anxiety and anguish: Establish the unconscious cause of endogenous anguish (Fear of losing control of impulses, reactions to the anniversary of some significant event, separation anxiety, drugs or drugs, reactions to a severe superego, moral Masochism, etc.), Establish the continuity between immediate anguish-detonating and personal history, unconscious meaning of the external event, provide structure to the patient, interpret the negation, encourage the cathartic expression of the effects and ideation associated with the anguish.

Pharmacology. As discussed in the section on biological causes of Generalized Anxiety Disorder, for the pharmacological treatment of this disease, the use of drugs that are widely used for the treatment of depression and mood disorders is used — specifically, selective serotonin reuptake inhibitors (SSRIs), related to the balance of GABA neurotransmitters.

Behavioral Cognitive Therapy. This therapeutic approach allows identifying and modifying the dysfunctional, automatic or irrational thoughts that have allowed the individual to react in an unadaptable way to stressful situations, establishing strategies of exposure and systematic desensitization that allow changing these behavior patterns.

Support Network. This network includes direct relatives and friendships of the person, contacts of the psychotherapist, emergency care centers, etc. As well as people who can take care of the children of these patients, in cases where they are in nervous breakdown or anxiety.

Agoraphobia

Agoraphobia literally means fear of open spaces. But agoraphobic, this disorder occurs more often among women than men, is characterized by anxiety that appears where it is difficult to escape or get help. As a result, there is an almost permanent avoidance of many situations, such as being alone inside or outside the home; sites with lots of people, mix with people; travel by car, bus, or plane; or find yourself on a bridge or in an elevator. Some agoraphobes can be exposed to these situations if they are accompanied. This disorder leads to a deterioration in the ability to travel or carry out domestic responsibilities, such as going to the supermarket or taking children to the doctor.

Agoraphobia may or may not be accompanied by:

Crisis of anguish

That the DSM-IV defines as the "temporary and isolated appearance of intense fear or discomfort, accompanied by four (or more) of the following symptoms, which start abruptly and reach their maximum expression in the first 10 min:

(1) palpitations, heart-shaking or elevation of heart rate

(2) sweating

(3) tremors or shaking

(4) feeling short of breath or breathless

(5) choking sensation

(6) tightness or chest discomfort

(7) nausea or abdominal discomfort

(8) instability, dizziness or fainting

(9) derealization (feeling of unreality) or depersonalization (being separated from oneself)

(10) fear of losing control or going crazy

(11) fear of dying

(12) paresthesia (sensation of numbness or tingling)

(13) chills or suffocations "

Panic disorder

The term "agoraphobia" is used here with a broader meaning than the original and that used even in some countries. It includes not only the fears of open places but also others related to them, such as fears of crowds and the difficulty of being able to escape immediately to a safe place (usually the home). The term encompasses a set of related phobias, sometimes overlapping, including fear of leaving home, going into stores or stores, crowds, public places and traveling only on trains, buses or planes. Although the severity of anxiety and the intensity of avoidance behavior are variable, this is the most disabling of phobic disorders, and some individuals become completely confined in their home. Many patients are terrified to think about the possibility of fainting or being alone, without help, in public. The experience of the lack of an immediate exit is one of the key features of many of the situations that induce agoraphobia. Most of those affected are women, and the disorder generally begins at the beginning of adult life. Depressive and obsessive symptoms and social phobias are often present, but they do not predominate in the clinical picture. In the absence of effective treatment, agoraphobia usually becomes chronic, although its intensity may be fluctuating.

Guidelines for diagnosis

To satisfy a definitive diagnosis, all the following conditions are required:

a) the symptoms, psychological or vegetative, are primary manifestations of anxiety and not secondary to other symptoms, such as delusional or obsessive ideas

b) this anxiety is limited or predominates in at least two of the following situations: crowds, public places, traveling away from home or traveling alone and

c) avoidance of the phobic situation is a prominent feature.

Differential diagnosis

It should be remembered that some agoraphobes experience very little anxiety because they are able to avoid their phobic situations. The presence of other symptoms such as depression, depersonalization, obsessive symptoms, and social phobias does not invalidate the diagnosis, as long as they are not predominant in the clinical picture. However, if the patient was already clearly depressed when the phobic symptoms first appeared, the most appropriate diagnosis may be a depressive episode. The latter is more frequent in cases of late onset.

Its essential characteristic is the presence of recurrent crises of serious anxiety (panic) not limited to any situation or set of particular circumstances. They are, therefore, unpredictable. As in other anxiety disorders, the predominant symptoms vary from case to case, but the sudden onset of palpitations, precordial pain, suffocation, dizziness or vertigo and feeling of unreality (depersonalization or derealization) are frequent. Almost constantly, there is a secondary fear of dying, losing control, or going crazy. Each crisis usually lasts only a few minutes but may last longer.

Both the frequency and the course of the disorder, which predominates in women, are quite variable. Often the fear and the vegetative symptoms of the attack grow in such a way that those who suffer them end up leaving, escaping, from where they are. If this takes place in a specific situation, for example, on a bus or in a crowd, as a consequence, the patient may, in the future, try to avoid that situation. Similarly, frequent and unpredictable panic attacks lead to a fear of being alone or going to public places. A panic attack is often followed by a persistent fear of having another panic attack.

Guidelines for diagnosis

In this classification, panic attacks that occur in a consolidated phobic situation are considered an expression of the severity of the phobia, and it has a preference for diagnosis. Panic disorder is the primary diagnosis only in the absence of any of the F40 phobias.

For a definitive diagnosis, there must be several serious attacks of vegetative anxiety at least during the period of one month:

a) in circumstances in which there is no objective danger

b) they should not be presented only in known or foreseeable situations and

c) in the period between crises, the individual must also be relatively free of anxiety, although mild anticipatory anxiety is common.

Differential diagnosis

Episodes should be distinguished from the panic that occurs in clear phobic disorders, as already mentioned. Panic attacks may be secondary to a depressive disorder, especially in males. The panic disorder should not be the main diagnosis if the patterns of depressive disorder are simultaneously satisfied.

Obsessive-Compulsive Disorder (OCD)

People with obsessive-compulsive behaviors have unwanted thoughts (obsessions) to which they feel the need to react (compulsions).

To help diagnose obsessive-compulsive disorder (OCD), mental health professionals use the fifth edition of the Diagnostic and Statistical Manual of Mental Disorders (DSM-5) of the American Psychiatric Association.

Below we present the diagnostic criteria in a summarized manner. Please keep in mind that they are here only for you to report and that they should not be used to self-diagnose. If you have concerns about any of the symptoms listed, you should consult with a trained health care provider experienced in the diagnosis and treatment of OCD.

Obsessions are defined according to the following two aspects:

Thoughts, impulses, or mental images that are constantly repeated. These thoughts, impulses, or mental images are unwanted and cause a lot of anxiety or stress.

The person who has these thoughts, impulses, or mental images tries to ignore them or make them disappear.

Compulsions are defined according to the following two aspects:

Behaviors (for example, washing hands, placing things in a specific order or revising something over and over again as when constantly verifying if a door is closed) or thoughts (for example, praying) , count numbers or repeat words in silence) that are repeated again and again or according to certain rules that must be followed strictly so that the obsession disappears.

The person feels that the purpose of these behaviors or thoughts is to prevent or reduce the anguish or to avoid a feared situation or event. However, these behaviors or thoughts are unrelated to reality or are clearly exaggerated.

In addition, the following conditions must be met:

Obsessions or compulsions consume a lot of time (more than one hour per day) or cause intense anguish or interfere significantly with the person's daily activities.

The symptoms are not due to the use of medications, other drugs, or another condition.

If the person has another disorder at the same time, the obsessions or compulsions cannot be related only to the symptoms of the additional disorder. For example, for the diagnosis of OCD, a person suffering an eating disorder should also have obsessions or compulsions that are not related only with food.

The diagnosis should also indicate whether the person with OCD understands that the obsessive-compulsive thoughts may not be true, or if they are convinced that they are true (for example, someone may know that it is not necessary to check the stove [kitchen] 30 times , but feel that you must do it anyway).

The diagnosis should also indicate whether a person with OCD has or has had a tic disorder. People with OCD and those with tic disorders tend to differentiate themselves from those without a history of tic disorders with respect to their symptoms, the presence of other disorders and the way in which OCD manifests itself in the family.

To make the diagnosis of Obsessive-Compulsive Disorder, the specialists are based on the diagnostic criteria of the DSM-V or the ICD-10, two classifications of diseases agreed by specialists of different nationalities and recognized prestige.

Remember that you cannot and should not self-diagnosed. Only an expert health professional is able to do it with rigor and reliability. When a person is worried about their health or normality, they usually identify with symptoms or diseases that they do not have or confuse them with other possible ones.

Obsessions are defined by 1, 2, 3, and 4:

1. thoughts, impulses or images and recurrent persistent that is experienced at some point in the disorder as intrusive and inappropriate, and cause significant anxiety or discomfort

2. thoughts, impulses or images are not reduced to simple excessive concerns about real-life problems

3. the person tries to ignore or suppress these thoughts, impulses or images or to neutralize with other thoughts or acts

4. the person recognizes that these thoughts, impulses or obsessional images are the product of your mind (not imposed as a thought insertion)

Compulsions are defined by 1 and 2:

1. behaviors (e.g., hand washing, putting things in order, checking) or mental acts (e.g., praying, count or repeat words in silence) of a repetitive nature, which the individual is forced to perform in response to an obsession or according to certain rules that must strictly follow

2. The objective of these behaviors or mental operations is the prevention or reduction of discomfort or the prevention of some negative event or situation; however, these behaviors or mental operations are either not realistically

connected with what they intend to neutralize or prevent, or they are clearly excessive.

At some point during the course of the disorder, the person has recognized that these obsessions or compulsions are excessive or irrational.

Note: This point is not applicable to children.

Obsessions or compulsions cause significant clinical discomfort, represent a waste of time (they take more than 1 hour a day) or interfere markedly with the daily routine of the individual, their work (or academic) relationships or their social life.

If there is another disorder, the content of obsessions or compulsions is not limited to it (e.g., concerns about food in an eating disorder, hair pulling in trichotillomania, concern about one's appearance in body dysmorphic disorder, concern about drugs in a substance use disorder, concern about having a serious illness in hypochondria, concern about the sexual needs or fantasies in a paraphilia or repetitive feelings of guilt in major depressive disorder).

The disorder is not due to the direct physiological effects of a substance (e.g., drugs, drugs) or a medical illness.

The essential characteristic of this disorder is the presence of obsessive thoughts or recurrent compulsive acts. The obsessive thoughts are ideas, images, or mental impulses that burst again and again into the mental activity of the individual, in a stereotyped way. They tend to be always unpleasant (because of their violent or obscene content, or simply because they are perceived as meaningless) and the sufferer usually tries, usually without success, to resist them. They are, however, perceived as one's own thoughts, although they are involuntary and often repulsive. Compulsive acts or rituals are stereotyped forms of behavior that are repeated over and over again. They are not pleasurable by themselves, nor do they give rise to useful activities by themselves. For the patient, they have the function of preventing an objectively improbable event from taking place. It is usually rituals to conjure up the one who takes damage from someone or can produce it to others. Often, although not always, this behavior is recognized by the patient as meaningless or ineffective and makes repeated attempts to resist it. In cases of a long evolution, resistance may have been reduced to a minimum level. A certain degree of anxiety is almost always present. There is an intimate relationship between obsessive symptoms, especially obsessive thoughts, and depression. Patients with obsessive-compulsive disorders often have depressive symptoms, and in patients suffering from a recurrent depressive disorder, obsessive thoughts often occur during their episodes of depression. In both situations, the increase or decrease in the severity of depressive symptoms is usually accompanied by parallel changes in the severity of the obsessive symptoms.

Obsessive-compulsive disorder is as frequent in men as it is in women, and the basic personality tends to have prominent features. The beginning is usually in childhood or at the beginning of adult life. The course is variable and, in the absence of significant depressive symptoms, tends more to chronic evolution.

Guidelines for diagnosis

For a definitive diagnosis, they must be present and be a major source of distress or disability for most days for at least two successive weeks, obsessive symptoms, compulsive acts, or both.

Obsession symptoms should have the following characteristics:

- They are recognized as thoughts or own impulses.

- There is an ineffective resistance to at least one of the thoughts or acts, although others are present to which the patient no longer resists.

- The idea or the realization of the act should not be in themselves pleasurable (the simple relief of tension or anxiety should not be considered pleasant in this sense).

- The thoughts, images, or impulses must be repeated and annoying.

- Obsessive-compulsive disorder can manifest itself:

- With the predominance of thoughts or obsessive ruminations

They can take the form of ideas, mental images, or impulses to act. Its content is very variable, but almost always accompanied by subjective discomfort. For example, a woman may be tormented by the fear of not being able to resist at some point the impulse to kill the beloved child, or by the obscene or blasphemous and alien quality of a recurrent mental image. Sometimes ideas are simply banal about an endless and almost philosophical consideration of imponderable alternatives. This indecisive consideration of alternatives is an important element in many other obsessive ruminations and is often accompanied by an inability to make decisions, even the most trivial, but necessary in everyday life.

The relationship between obsessive ruminations and depression is particularly intimate, and the diagnosis of the obsessive-compulsive disorder will be chosen only when the ruminations appear or persist in the absence of a depressive disorder.

With Predominance of Compulsive Acts (Obsessive Rituals)

Most compulsive acts are related to cleanliness (particularly hand washing), with repeated checks to ensure that a potentially dangerous situation has been avoided, or with neatness and the order. In the manifest behavior, there is usually a fear of being the object or cause of danger, and the ritual is an ineffective or symbolic attempt to conjure that danger. Compulsive rituals can take many hours each day and are often accompanied by a marked inability to make decisions and slow down. Together, they are as common in one sex as in the other, but ritual hand washing is more common in women, and slowing without repetition is more common in men.

Rituals are less closely related to depression than obsessive thoughts and respond more easily to behavior modification therapies.

With Mixed Thoughts and Obsessive Acts

Most patients with an obsessive-compulsive disorder have both obsessive thoughts and compulsions. This subcategory should be used when both are equally intense, as is often the case, although it is useful to specify only one when clearly highlighted since thoughts and actions may respond to different treatments.

Dissociative Disorders

- Dissociative disorders can be explored in a specific way so that we can make a positive diagnosis and not by exclusion.

- If we use the appropriate evaluation methods, the dissociative disorders will show a significant frequency, and many people who have been receiving other diagnoses can be correctly diagnosed.

- There is a set of traumatic-based pathologies, in which simple PTSD is on one side of the spectrum, and dissociative disorders and complex post-traumatic stress disorders are at the opposite extreme and more severe.

- Dissociative disorders can be treated, and the treatment must be specific and adapted to them. With this approach, the prognosis of these people improves considerably.

Regarding the diagnosis, 94% of patients with DID do not have obvious symptoms, being more obvious the co-morbid pathologies such as anxiety, depression, or substance abuse. The fact that the manifestations of DID are subtle and discontinuous makes diagnosis difficult if we do not explore the internal struggles in the patient's mind.

Sometimes several queries are necessary to perceive transitions from one part to another.

The ego states are "organized systems of conduct and experience that are linked by a common principle and that are separated by more or less permeable limits." Among these states, there are no rigid amnesiac barriers as in the TID, nor do they normally take control of the behavior.

When we collect the background and ask about problems in childhood and adolescence, the person can tell what they remember, but it is impossible to tell us what they cannot remember, especially if there is amnesia regarding a whole period. We will need a deep biographical exploration.

We also miss unnoticed lapses or memory gaps, described by patients as memory problems, which we attribute to concentration difficulties and which may be times when a mental state different from the PAN "has taken control of the behavior, presenting complete amnesia between both states." This symptom would be, according to several authors, the most common in the TID. Therefore, if we find symptoms of amnesia, we must deepen the exploration.

The same will happen if we find a dissociative leak or symptoms of depersonalization: we should explore further to assess whether we should diagnose these disorders as such, as part of other tables (symptoms of depersonalization are common in several psychiatric pictures) or if they are part of a TID.

Dissociation is effective against trauma when there is no way to avoid it by allowing an escape from an intolerable level of suffering. However, in the future, the person with dissociative reactions will not know how to protect themselves from situations in which they could do so.

Amnesia allows us to continue living as if nothing had happened. One of the mechanisms that would work would be the "state-dependent memory." When the person is in this state of mind, these memories will be more accessible, but may not be when the mental state is different.

Amnesia may be due to a primary structural dissociation or may be part of a tertiary dissociation (TID), in which case the parties that deal with daily life will have amnesia about the traumas experienced. When a different mental state is activated, motivated by an emotional reaction of anger or sadness, the traumatic memories will be present.

Amnestic barriers can also be constituted to be able to love an abusive or abusing parent at times when he is not abusing, even if he is hated at the time of the abuse. In the most serious case, dissociated identities will be generated. These can sometimes represent introjections of the abusive figures and interact with the main personality as the abuser did, becoming persecutory parties. This should be, according to the author, that "the only available model of strength, power, influence over others and control over something is precisely the figure that, in one way or another, is assaulting him. In the world in which this individual has grown, the only possible options are to be a defenseless victim or a powerful aggressor. "The aggressive part, therefore, would be generated as a need to protect oneself, later becoming persecutory in the system. The elements of both parts, essential for life, appear separately, oscillating the person from one to another according to the mental state that is activated.

On the other hand, it is not about trauma alone. The author argues that the severity of the disorder will depend to a large extent on the bond of attachment established with the caretakers. If there was at least one secure attachment link, the forecast is much more favorable. This can "teach the child that negativity can be supported and overcome," which would allow the development of resilience.

The dissociation would be related to the type of disorganized attachment. The creatures with this attachment pattern would then tend to see the caregiver as helpless and themselves as bad, while at other times the caregiver would be aggressive, and they would be vulnerable. Other times, they will be in the role of rescuing the helpless adult. Thus, "multiple models of the self, which are incoherent or incompatible," would be constructed. This will generate a predisposition to dissociative symptoms.

If serious trauma is added to all this, the chances of developing a DID increase.

Treatment

Many of the therapies received by these patients are based on a misdiagnosis that places them in other categories and is therefore treated as schizophrenic, limits In other cases, although dissociative symptoms are observed, professionals decide not to give them importance, thinking that if they are not taken care of they will be extinguished as if they were attention calls.

However, the therapies that have shown greater effectiveness are those that work specifically with these symptoms.

- Address fragmentation: This would be the central aspect of the treatment

- The guideline should first be to achieve safety and stability in the life of the patient, to then move on to the second phase of work with the trauma and, finally, to address the integration of the dissociated parts.

- Establish an adequate therapeutic relationship. Due to the problems suffered in the attachment bond by these patients, they will have similar relational difficulties to patients with BPD.

Due to the attachment problems, the patient will also have a series of negative expectations towards us, such as that we will want to dominate him, that we will end up abandoning him, that we only want to know his secret, that we will harm him sooner or later, or that we will despise him when we know him. better and all this must be redefined by us as an adaptive precaution, asking for permission for each step of the treatment, always checking the reaction of each of the parties and showing a secure link where it is unconditionally accepted and not judged as good or bad, rather, it is intended that the adaptive resources that each party possesses can be used in another way.

Regarding the stages of the treatment for the treatment of trauma, first is stabilization and strengthening of the patient, then memory processing and the final phase is reconnection.

Phase 1. Stabilization

In this phase, we must "establish a good therapeutic alliance and educate patients about their problems."

Psychoeducation will be applied to make sense of the patient's symptoms, explaining the connection between the symptoms and the experiences lived. Furthermore, from the beginning, it will be stressed in the therapeutic alliance that we accept all the mental states of the patient, including the most negative ones, in order to teach her how to accept herself. Often, we will have to negotiate with the aggressive parties from the first sessions so that they do not boycott the treatment or generate more damage. However, as the author clarifies, we must not assume as true the vision of the patient, who can have demonized and want to annihilate. Since they are part of the same person, we must show them that they are not the enemy, but a fundamental part of their mind and that we will take their opinion into account during the treatment. In this way, in the therapy, we will establish a functioning of negotiation between the parties and not of the struggle between them.

We reproduce here because of its clinical interest, a fragment of clinical intervention. It is a patient who hears a voice asking him to commit aggressive acts.

Personality Disorders

Personality disorders encompass a wide range of alterations that manifest themselves in all areas of the person's activity. Looking for a simile, we would say that they would become our psychological mutation.

Personality is constituted by a set of traits that define us and differentiate us from others.

With personality, we refer to that invisible reality that leads us to behave to everyone in a different way and makes that while I like basketball, eggs with ham and literature, there are those who prefer soccer, tacos and skiing.

One of the most classic definitions and still used today affirms that personality must be understood as persistent patterns of ways of perceiving, relating and thinking about the environment and oneself.

This invisible reality has as raw material all the experiences that we accumulate from the maternal womb. Its moment of inception has been signaled around three years when self-consciousness appears, or what is the same, when we discover that we exist as a reality independent of the rest of the world.

But that personality that we are can take unforeseen and undesirable ways. Then the disorders of the personality are gestated, which would be an alteration that is established in our own essence, in our own identity.

The definition of most recent personality disorders states that it is:

A lasting pattern of behavior and inner experience that deviates markedly from the expectations of the individual's culture, is pervasive and inflexible, has its beginnings in early adolescence or adulthood, It is stable with the passage of time and induces distress or deterioration.

Personality traits become pathological when they are inflexible and misaligned, not allowing us to function properly in the different significant contexts of our life (family, work, school, etc.).

Antisocial Personality Disorder

This is a pattern of behavior based on hostility, aggression, and manipulation. They are usually liars, impulsive, and usually cannot be trusted.

They are people with a negative view of themselves that feeds on the insufficiency and inhibition in the establishment of intimate relationships with the rest of the people.

They have a high level of anxiety and always feel inferior, unattractive, and often ashamed of themselves. Avoidant disorder is roughly a pathological form of shyness.

Borderline Personality Disorder

In this case, self-concept is widely affected. This is characterized by its fragility and by how easily it is altered. Such anomalies manifest themselves in a poorly structured identity and in chronic feelings of emptiness.

They are emotionally unstable, and it is very difficult for them to maintain lasting intimate relationships.

Schizotypal Personality Disorder

They have marked social deficits and do not manage to feel comfortable in their interpersonal relationships. They also tend to have eccentric characteristics in the way they dress or in their strange habits and beliefs, such as having powers or predicting the future.

Cases of de-compensation may present pseudo illusions and sensory illusions, among other symptoms that place them on the edge of a psychotic level.

Sexual Disorders

In our society, sexual behaviors continue to be a taboo subject, which is why many doubts remain regarding the different problems and disorders related to sex. What is a sexual disorder? What is the difference between a dysfunction and a disorder? How can I treat my sexual problems?

If all these doubts appear in your mind, we recommend you continue reading this interesting Psychology-Online article. In it, you will find an extensive study of sexual dysfunctions and the listing of symptoms of sexual disorders according to the DSM-V: the most used diagnostic manual in psychology.

Sexual Disorders According To Psychology

Luckily, psychology has tried to collect all possible information related to sexual behavior and orientations. From Freud's psychoanalysis to Kinsey's sexual orientation scale, there have been many experts who have tried to study the human behavior of the sexual act.

List of common sexual disorders and their symptoms

Some of the most common sexual disorders and what are their diagnostic criteria:

1. Sexual Dysfunctions

In order to diagnose the sexual dysfunctions that we have mentioned throughout the article, we must comply with the following criteria:

There are no organic pathology / or substances produce discomfort accused difficulties in interpersonal relationships

Present in most sexual relationships (70-80%)

Persistence at least 6 months

2. Hypoactive sexual desire

Decrease (or absence) of fantasies and sexual activity desires persistently or recurrently. The judgment of deficiency or absence must be made by the clinician, taking into account factors that, as the age, sex, and context of the individual's life, affect sexual activity.

Hypoactive sexual disorder causes marked discomfort or interpersonal relationship difficulties.

The sexual disorder is not better explained by the presence of another disorder (except another sexual dysfunction) and is not due exclusively to the direct physiological effects of a substance (e.g., drugs, alcohol) or to a medical illness.

3. Sex aversion

Persistent or recurrent extreme aversion towards, and with avoidance of, all (or practically all) genital sexual contacts with a sexual partner.

The alteration causes marked discomfort or difficulties in interpersonal relationships.

The sexual disorder is not better explained by the presence of another disorder (except another sexual disorder).

4. Paraphilias

Non-normative sexual behaviors in which the patient shows absolute dependence on that object or behavior to obtain pleasure.

Currently, the term addiction is also admitted.

Some of the most common paraphilias are: exhibitionism, fetishism, frotteurism, sexual masochism, and sexual sadism.

Psychiatry of sexual disorders

Their dichotomous vision of this type of disorder (sexual or non-sexual dysfunction) has been criticized since sexuality, and sexual functioning seems to adjust better to a continuum of individual and interpersonal satisfaction (see Wincze and Carey, 1991). In the same way, the differentiation of the psychogenic subtypes has been questioned. (see LoPiccolo, 1992; Mohr and Beutler, 1990).

For its part, the most recent classification of the World Health Organization, the ICD-10 (WHO, 1992) shows a remarkable parallelism with the classification of the APA, including among the non-organic sexual dysfunctions the following:

- Excessive sexual impulse (which is the main novelty, since this diagnostic category is not included in the DSM-IV).
- Absence or loss of sexual desire.
- Rejection and absence of sexual pleasure.
- Failure in the genital response.
- Orgasmic dysfunction
- Premature ejaculation
- Non-organic dyspareunia
- Non-organic vaginismus
- Other sexual dysfunctions

These classifications, depending on the phases of the sexual response, do not obviate the diagnostic overlaps. In fact, overlap and comorbidity are frequent. Thus, for example, a study with 588 patients (men and women) diagnosed with hypoactive TDS, found that 41% of women and 47% of men had at least one other sexual dysfunction

Conclusions

Despite the limitations of the diagnosis based on the DSM-IV or the ICD-10, it is clear that they are widely accepted classification systems and that they have a relatively accurate description of the type of symptoms or behaviors that are included.

Alternative DSM-5 Model for Personality Disorders

Apart from the classification to which the DSM already has accustomed us for personality disorders (PD), the DSM-5 proposes an alternative model, with aspects in common but with a greater dimensionality.

PD's are characterized by:

a) Difficulties in personal functioning, and

b) Pathological personality traits.

Therefore, for the diagnosis of PD, the evaluation of both aspects is required.

a) Regarding PERSONAL PERFORMANCE, it is required to show difficulties in 2 of the following 4 facets:

- In the functioning of the Self:

1) Identity

2) Self-direction

- In interpersonal functioning:

3) Empathy

4) Intimacy

Difficulties can be assessed with the LFPS scale (Scale of Personal Performance Level), which goes from "no or little difficulty" to "extreme difficulty," with a score of 0 to 4 respectively. For the diagnosis of PD, at least one severity level 2 (moderate) is necessary. The severity on this scale predicts whether the patient has more than one TD.

The personal functioning, in general, predicts the presence of a TD in the patient, while the psychopathological features that we see below, describe the characteristics of the most specific disorder.

b) Regarding the TRAITS OF PSYCHOPATHOLOGICAL PERSONALITY, define 5 traits or domains that are maladaptive variations of the Big Five, each with its distinctive facets:

1) Negative affect (vs. emotional stability in the other pole)

Facets:

- Emotional ability

- Anxiety

- Separation Anxiety

- Submission

- Hostility

- Perseveration

2) Disengagement or estrangement (vs. Extraversion)

Facets:

- Withdrawal

- Avoidance of intimacy

- Anhedonia

- Depression

- Restricted affect

- Suspicion

3) Antagonism (vs. Affability)

Facets:

- Manipulation

- Falsehood
- Grandiosity
- Search for attention
- Insensibility

4) Disinhibition (vs. conscience)

Facets:

- Irresponsibility
- Impulsivity
- Risk-taking
- Rigid perfectionism

5) Psychoticism (vs. lucidity)

Facets:

- Beliefs and experiences Unusual
- Eccentricity
- Cognitive and perceptual dysregulation (includes derealization, depersonalization, and dissociation)

These features can in measuring with the PID-5 (Personality Inventory for DSM-5). From the combination of traits are derived as specific disorders:

- Antisocial
- Avoider
- Limit
- Narcissistic
- Obsessive-compulsive
- Schizotypal

Also included is a diagnosis of "TP-specific trait," in which it is considered that a TP is present but not one in particular. The traits that are observed should be described.

Affective Episodes

At the diagnostic level, mood disorders start from the episode concept. The DSM-IV describes three types of affective episodes (depressive, manic and hypomanic), with the disorders defined in terms of the duration of these episodes and the combination of episodes observed (Vázquez & Sanz, 1995).

Major Depressive Episode

The major depressive episode is characterized by a depressed mood or a loss of interest or pleasure in almost all activities for at least 2 weeks and most of the day. In children and adolescents, the mood can be irritable instead of sad. In addition, the subject must experience at least four other symptoms that include changes in appetite or weight, sleep and psychomotor activity; lack of energy; feelings of undervaluation or guilt; difficulty in thinking, concentrating or making decisions, and recurrent thoughts of death or suicidal ideation, plans or attempts. The episode must be accompanied by significant clinical discomfort or social, occupational, or other important impairment of the individual's activity. In some subjects with mild episodes, the activity may seem normal, but at the cost of a very important effort.

The onset of symptoms

The symptoms of a major depressive episode usually develop over days or weeks, sometimes preceded by weeks or months of anxious symptoms and mild depressive symptoms. The duration of a major depressive episode is also variable; it is usual for an untreated episode to last 6 months or longer, regardless of the age of onset. In most cases, there is complete remission of symptoms and can return to normal functioning.

Between 20 and 30% of major depressive episodes partially remit, some depressive symptoms persist for months or even years, although not with such intensity and incapacitation. These people are more likely to suffer new depressive episodes.

Between 5-10%, the major depressive episode becomes chronic and can last 2 or more years.

Studies indicate that depressive episodes occur twice as often in women as in men. A significant proportion of women report a worsening of symptoms of the major depressive episode a few days before the onset of menstruation.

Manic Episode

A manic episode is defined by a specific period during which the mood is abnormal and persistently high, expansive or irritable. This period of abnormal mood should last at least 1 week (or less if hospitalization is required). Mood disturbance must be accompanied by at least three other symptoms of a list that include increased self-esteem or grandiosity, decreased need for sleep, verbose language, brain drain, distractibility, increased intentional activities or agitation psychomotor and excessive involvement in pleasant activities with a high potential to produce serious consequences.

The appearance of symptoms

The average age of onset of a first manic episode is in the first years of the third decade of life, but there are some cases of onset in adolescence and others that begin after 50 years. Manic episodes begin abruptly, with a rapid increase in symptoms in a few days. Frequently, manic episodes appear after psychosocial stress. The episodes usually last from a few weeks to several months and are shorter and with a more abrupt end than major depressive episodes. In many cases (50-60%) a major depressive episode precedes or immediately follows a manic episode, without there being an intermediate period of euthymia. If the manic episode occurs in the puerperal period, there may be an increased risk of recurrences in other puerperal periods, and the postpartum initiation specification should be applied.

Mixed Episode

A mixed episode is characterized by a period of time (of at least 1-week duration) in which almost every day the criteria are met for both a manic episode and a major depressive episode. The subject experiences moods that alternate rapidly (sadness, irritability, euphoria), accompanied by symptoms of a manic episode and a major depressive episode. The symptoms of presentation usually include agitation, insomnia, appetite alteration, psychotic symptoms, and suicidal ideation. The disturbance must be severe enough to cause significant social or occupational impairment or to require hospitalization or is characterized by the presence of psychotic symptoms. The disturbance is not due to the direct physiological effects of a substance (e.g., a drug, medication or other treatment) or to a medical illness (e.g., hyperthyroidism).

The onset of symptoms

Mixed episodes can arise from a manic episode or a depressive episode. For example, in a subject with 3 weeks of manic symptoms followed by 1 week of both manic and depressive symptoms, the diagnosis of bipolar I disorder, most recent manic episode, should be changed to that of bipolar I disorder, most recent mixed episode. Mixed episodes can last from weeks to several months and may remit to a period with few or no symptoms or progress to a major depressive episode. It is much less common for a mixed episode to evolve into a manic episode.

Hypomanic episode

A hypomanic episode is defined as a limited period during which there are an abnormal mood and persistently high, expansive or irritable that lasts at least 4 days. This period of abnormal mood should be accompanied by at least three other symptoms from a list that includes increased self-esteem or grandiosity (not delirious), decreased need for sleep, verbose language, brain drain, distractibility, increased intentional activities or psychomotor agitation and excessive involvement in pleasant activities with a high potential to produce serious consequences. If the mood is irritable (instead of elevated or expansive), there must be at least four of the above symptoms. The list of additional symptoms is identical to the one that defines a manic episode except that there can be no delusions and hallucinations.

The appearance of symptoms

In general, hypomanic episodes begin abruptly, with a rapid increase in symptoms in 1 or 2 days. The episodes usually last from a few weeks to several months and are shorter and with a more abrupt end than major depressive episodes. In many cases, the hypomanic episode may be preceded or followed by a major depressive episode. The available studies suggest that 5-15% of subjects with hypomania will end up having a manic episode.

Latest News On The Diagnostic and Statistical Manual of Mental Disorders

Recently, in May 2013, the American Academy of Psychiatry (AAP) presented the latest version of the DSM (Diagnostic and Statistical Manual of Mental Disorders). The previous version DSM-IV-TR was from 1994. The DSM was originally established to classify mental disorders and facilitate agreements between medical insurance companies. This last version has generated great controversy, since the British Association of Psychology has been against the application of an exclusively biomedical model for the understanding of mental disorders, because, as is known, psychological factors also influence its development. social. Even the National Institute of Mental Health (NIMH) has announced that it will stop using the DSM.

The DSM-5, in relation to the previous version of the DSM IV-TR, presents changes related to the organization of the disorders; since, these are established according to the sex, development and cultural characteristics of the patient, eliminating the multiaxial evaluation system, as it created artificial distinctions. But most substantial, it refers to the novelties in the specific diagnoses of the different disorders.

Next, the most relevant modifications for clinical practice at a general level and specifically in ADHD are exposed.

New disorders have been incorporated, such as disruptive emotional dysregulation disorder (Disruptive Mood Dysregulation Disorder). It is characterized by children with recurrent tantrums and disproportionate in intensity and duration, 3 or more times per week for more than a year. In addition, persistently show an angry and irritable mood, present in at least two environments (home, school, or with classmates). They are children with frequent episodes of a great lack of control in their behavior. The beginning of the picture is before 10 years, and the diagnosis will not be made before 6 or after 18 years. This new category arises after a wide debate on the suitability of the diagnosis of bipolar disorder in childhood and the opinion of most experts about the increase in this diagnosis in children.

Also, binge eating disorder (Binge Eating Disorder) has been incorporated when eating more than 12 times excessively during a period of 3 months (in the DSM-IV it did not have a category of disorder). It involves adjusting impulsive intake behaviors to clinical reality and establishing the appropriate clinical importance of these behaviors.

Likewise, the excoriation disorder when there is a compulsive scratching of the skin. Scratching is excluded due to somatic diseases such as cutaneous atopy. Hoarding disorder was previously considered a symptom of obsessive-compulsive disorder but is currently considered a disorder by itself. It is defined as persistent difficulty in detaching objects, regardless of their value. The premenstrual dysphoric disorder is one of the categories that has caused more debate because of doubts about its psychopathological significance. Transsexuality is no longer considered a mental disorder.

Autism spectrum disorder (ASD) comprises four diagnoses that were separated in the DSM-IV: autistic disorder, Asperger's disorder, childhood disintegrative disorder, and pervasive developmental disorder. ASD is characterized by:

1. deficit in communication and social interaction; and

2. restricted behavior, interests, and activities, repetitive and stereotyped. When there is only the presence of the first, then the diagnosis is of social communication disorder. Therefore, well-established diagnoses disappear, such as Asperger's syndrome.

With respect to anxiety disorders, dissociative disorders, obsessive-compulsive disorder, and post-traumatic stress disorder, previously unified under the same heading, are currently described in separate sections to legitimize their distinct character.

Regarding post-traumatic stress disorders, the DSM-5 includes four groups of symptoms for diagnosis: re-experimentation, excitement, avoidance, and persistent negative alterations in cognition and mood. In addition, the level of development is taken into account since there are different diagnostic criteria for children under 6 years of age.

Major depressive disorder includes two categories to more accurately reflect suicidal ideation: suicidal behavior disorder and non-suicidal self-harm.

In relation to grief, in the DSM-5, the diagnosis of depression in the first two months of grief is not excluded, as it happened in the DSM-IV. It has been eliminated that the normal thing is that it lasts 2 months since in clinical practice it usually lasts from 1 to 2 years. Also, it is considered to be an adverse psychosocial factor that can trigger major depression in a predisposed individual, generally occurring shortly after the loss.

For anorexia nervosa, the requirement for the presence of amenorrhea to adapt it to clinical reality has been eliminated.

Regarding the substance use disorder, this section in the DSM-5 covers the substance abuse disorders and substance dependence of the DSM-IV. In addition, a new category has been created to collect behavioral addictions, including pathological gambling (previously unclassified impulse control disorders).

Finally, regarding attention deficit hyperactivity disorder (ADHD), the most prominent changes are:

- It is classified as a neurodevelopmental disorder.
- Its existence is recognized in adulthood, requiring one less symptom (5 out of 9 of inattention and 5 out of 9 of hyperactivity-impulsivity).
- Age of onset before age 12 (previously it was before age 7).
- The presentation of symptoms is trans situational, that is, several symptoms in different environments.
- At least two different informants are required, preferably a parent and a teacher.
- The comorbid diagnosis with ASD is accepted.
- The subtypes in the DSM-5 are called presentations: combined, with a predominance of attention deficit, with a predominance of hyperactive-impulsive.

In this category, the most important changes are established in recognition of the disorder as an entity that can last a lifetime, and that is not only a childhood disorder, the possibility of being diagnosed in a situation of comorbidity with autism spectrum disorders. and the delay in age, in which the symptoms must be present to establish the diagnosis. This last aspect is very important since there are patients who, due to the influence of factors such as a high intellectual quotient or cultural and educational support, etc., can develop the disorder in later ages.

As conclusions, the new classification provides few novelties with respect to the previous classification and also the consensus among the organizations and experts that have participated in its elaboration has been less. Although there are categories that can improve the diagnostic systematics, others have been the subject of ample debate, and we will have to wait for their use in daily practice to verify the robustness of the suggested criteria.

Fetal Alcohol Spectrum Disorder

As a result of prenatal alcohol exposure, Fetal Alcohol Spectrum Disorder (FASD) is characterized by a series of physical, organic, and related symptoms. Neurological development Symptoms that are permanent and irreversible can vary from mild to severe and carry high social costs. The condition in the Central Nervous System may include structural abnormalities and neurological and / or functional alterations.

It is essential to diagnose the FASD in order to connect those affected with adequate services and resources and to ensure that they and their families receive good support to manage the difficulties associated with these disabilities. It is essential to make a multidisciplinary evaluation (psychology, medicine, speech therapy, therapy,) and as complete as possible. Early recognition can capitalize on neuronal plasticity, and early intervention and continued care can maximize the development potential of children.

Under the umbrella of the FASD is the Neurobehavioral Disorder associated with the Prenatal Alcohol Exposure (ND-PAE), which was introduced in the DSM-5 manual as "Another neurological development disorder specified" and as "Condition for further study" (315.8, F88). The diagnosis of ND-PAE covers the behavioral and mental health aspects of the FASD with and without physical dysmorphology. It requires prenatal exposure to alcohol and deterioration in three functional domains: neurocognitive, self-regulating, and adaptive. The deficits associated with these domains are heterogeneous and complex, and there is no single standard applied to all those affected (Doyle, LR & Mattson, SN (2015).) Neurobehavioral Disorder Associated with Prenatal Alcohol Exposure (ND-PAE): Review of Evidence and Guidelines for Assessment, Curr Dev Devord, Rep., 2 (3): 175-186).

Neurocognitive impairment should show deficits in at least one of the following areas: global intellectual performance, executive functioning, learning, memory, and visuospatial reasoning. Deterioration in self-regulation requires deficits in one or more of the following areas: mood or behavior regulation, attention, and impulse control. Deterioration in adaptive functioning requires deficits in two or more of the following areas, specifying one in the first two: communication, social interaction, daily life skills, and motor skills.

Early traumas (physical and / or psychological events and abuse or neglect) can trigger serious behavioral problems that overlap with the FASD, such as diagnoses of conduct disorder, oppositional defiant disorder, anxiety or depression.

Children of foster care and adoption, especially of international adoption (with a prevalence of FASD that can reach 50%), can often suffer early traumas, separation and lack of attention and early stimulation. Therefore, they have a notorious probability of a comorbid diagnosis with FASD of reactive attachment disorder or post-traumatic stress disorder after abandonment.

In the FASD problems of attention and impulsivity arise from the prenatal exposure to alcohol, but there is the possibility that the FASD is diagnosed only as ADHD, being essential to act responsibly and diligently for the differential diagnosis. Between FASD and ADHD, there are differences in their manifestations. In FASD, there are higher rates of social behavior problems that result from difficulties in social cognition, emotional processing, etc. and there may also be more problems concerning overstimulation than in ADHD. In the latter, there is more difficulty in concentration and sustained attention than in FASD. In patients with FASD, medication for the symptoms of ADHD can produce unexpected results and often are not effective.

All these comorbid disorders, described with the FASD, together with others of different nature (intellectual disability, sleep abnormalities, language disorder, learning problems, bipolar disorder, some features of autism, specific phobias) are presented in very different This diversity of alterations together with the great ignorance of the FASD in the mental health professionals, favor that the FASD be diagnosed exclusively and / or erroneously as comorbid conditions, contributing to the amplification of the existing damages in the affected ones and provoking new damages.

With age, the deficiencies exposed for the three functional domains are shown differently and overlap with the other comorbid disorders, in such a way that they can promote a series of secondary conditions and disabilities, such as mental health problems, school failure, problems with justice, inappropriate sexual behavior, addiction to alcohol or drugs, dependent life, problems with employment, or leading to suicide. Therefore, early diagnosis and treatment can reduce the risk of these additional disabilities and their adverse outcomes.

Made in United States
Orlando, FL
16 July 2024

49071522R00117